James B. Fry

New York and the Conscription of 1863

A chapter in the history of the civil war

James B. Fry

New York and the Conscription of 1863
A chapter in the history of the civil war

ISBN/EAN: 9783337410605

Printed in Europe, USA, Canada, Australia, Japan

Cover: Foto ©ninafisch / pixelio.de

More available books at **www.hansebooks.com**

NEW YORK

AND

THE CONSCRIPTION

OF 1863

A CHAPTER IN THE HISTORY OF THE CIVIL WAR

BY

JAMES B. FRY

RETIRED

ASSISTANT ADJUTANT-GENERAL, WITH RANK OF COLONEL
BREVET MAJOR-GENERAL U. S. ARMY
LATE PROVOST-MARSHAL GENERAL OF THE UNITED STATES

NEW YORK & LONDON
G. P. PUTNAM'S SONS
The Knickerbocker Press
1885

NEW YORK

AND

THE CONSCRIPTION.

The New York Herald of November 4, 1878, gave an account of an interview at Deerfield Farm, near Utica, New York, between one of its correspondents and Ex-Governor Horatio Seymour, from which the following is an extract :

"A REMINISCENCE OF THE DRAFT.

" When an enrolment for draft was ordered during the rebellion," he proceeded, " every consideration of justice and duty called for its honest execution. It was a lottery for life, and it was a great crime to make it unfair. When it was completed it was found to be cruelly unjust. Not only were the quotas asked of New York as a whole more than those of any other Atlantic State, but this excess was imposed in a cruel way upon the city. * * * The matter was the subject of a correspondence with President Lincoln which resulted in the appointment by the President of two men and of one man by myself as Governor to conduct an inquiry. The two Commissioners named by the President were from other States, were officers of the army, and were naturally inclined to distrust the charge of unfairness. They spent a long time in a laborious search into the facts. Rising above all prejudices, they decided that the quotas of New York and Brooklyn were erroneous and excessive and should be reduced." * * *

" The riot was caused not only by an unjust enrolment but by the way the draft was made. It was begun without giving any notice to General Wool in command of the United States forces, to Mayor Opdyke, or to the Governor of the State. It was at a time when the city regiments were in Pennsylvania volunteering to defend that State from the attack of Lee's army. The United States soldiers were withdrawn for the same purpose; and so far as military force was concerned, the city was left almost in a defenseless state."

The *New York Times* of August 18, 1879, contained a life * of Ex-Governor Horatio Seymour, from which the following is an extract :

" On Saturday, July 12, while he was at Long Branch, and still engaged in this work of providing for the defense of the coast, he was startled by a telegram informing him that the long-threatened and much dreaded conscription of men for the Union Army had been commenced in New York City. This telegram was a private one. Governor Seymour never received any official notification that the draft was to commence, or that it had commenced, nor was any such notification sent to Mr. Opdyke, the Mayor of the city, or to General Wool, the United States officer in command. Without any communication with those gentlemen, or with the Department of Police, * * * the Provost Marshal, at whose instance is to this day a mat-

---

* See Appendix A.

ter of doubt, commenced the draft. The drawing began on Saturday in a district where the enrolment was so excessive, so grossly unjust, that the Government caused it to be changed. * * * It has been claimed that there was in all this a deep-seated design for political purposes, to force a portion of the community into such excesses as would make it necessary to declare the Empire City under martial law. This claim has not been justified, but that the Provost Marshals, or those behind them, by their action in the matter, threw prudence, propriety, and common sense to the winds, there can, in view of subsequent events, be no doubt. * * * On Sunday night, when he first received word that the draft was actually in progress, he tried to make his way to the city, but found that he could not do so. The next morning at a very early hour he received a second telegram, informing him that serious disturbances were expected to follow the announcement of the conscription. Fearing the worst, and without having tasted food, he hurried to the Metropolis."

The foregoing extracts bear strong evidence of authenticity. They have stood for many years without disavowal or denial. In a book in which Governor Seymour occupies the first place, called *Twelve Americans*, by Howard Carroll, published by Harpers, in 1883, the statement from the *New York Times* given in the Appendix A, is substantially repeated. In the preface the author says : " It is particularly worthy of note, that the material for these sketches of their lives, was, in every case, obtained during long and frequent personal interviews with them. Originally the sketches appeared in comparatively meagre outline in the columns of the *New York Times.*" Unpleasant affairs in which the Governor's part was very important if not satisfactory, are thus again brought into notice. Lincoln and Stanton and Whiting and Dix and Canby and many others concerned are dead, but the records remain. Lest the allegations of bad judgment, neglect, crime, unfairness, grievous wrong, " throwing prudence, propriety, and common sense to the winds," etc., leveled by high authority against officers of the general government, pass unchallenged into history, it is proposed to make a review of the general subject in the light of official documents and well established facts, and leave the reader to draw conclusions and make comments.

To understand the occurrences discussed it is necessary to recall the state of affairs in the spring and summer of 1862. Let the Adjutant-General of New York bear witness upon that point. In his report to the Governor of the State, dated December 31, 1862 (the close of Governor Morgan's term and the beginning of Governor Seymour's), he says : " Without any general or formal call your Excellency was advised in a dispatch from the Adjutant-General of the Army of May 21st, that an additional force of three years' volunteers would be accepted, and a plan of organization was at once decided on and promulgated in General Orders 31, issued on the 23d. Owing, however, to the great demand for labor in the field and workshop no great progress was made, and on the 1st of July, more than a month after, although one hundred and fifty authorizations to raise companies had been issued, the aggregate of the enlistments did not exceed three thousand men. There was nothing of that eagerness to enter the service which had been manifested at previous periods, and it appeared as if the people had fallen into an apathy from which only an extraordinary effort could arouse them. Meanwhile, the most important events were transpiring. The losses sustained by our army in Virginia from sickness, and in the sanguinary engagements which had taken place on the Peninsula, had reduced it to a defensive attitude, and rendered its reinforcement or withdrawal a matter of necessity. In the West, notwithstanding the success of the military operations which terminated with the occupation of Corinth, the waste from disease and battle, and the necessity of occupying strategic points, had so much reduced the force available for field operations, that the Confederates, with numbers greatly augmented through a rigorous conscription, were preparing to assume the offensive in a series of movements which subsequently brought them to the banks of the Ohio and Potomac."

Such was the condition of affairs when, on the 28th of June, 1862, the Governors of the loyal States united in an appeal to the President to call upon the several States for more men. In response, the President, on July 2, 1862, issued his call for 300,000 volunteers. This was felt, in fact was known, to be the final effort to suppress the rebellion by voluntary military service. Every possible form of encouragement was adopted for the purpose of stimulating enlistments, and with some success in the State of New York and throughout the United States. But the demand for troops during the summer increased more rapidly than the supply, so that on the 4th of August the President issued his Proclamation for 300,000 *nine months' militia*, and the War Department followed the Proclamation with orders and instructions, under which the Governors of some of the States commenced a draft as ordered by the general Government on the 3d of September. At that date the military reverses of the season had culminated in the disastrous campaign of the army of Northern Virginia, under General Pope, and the prospect of raising troops became very gloomy. Of the 300,000 militia required only about 87,000 "were ever credited as having been drafted into the service under the call. This number was much reduced by desertion before the men could be got out of their respective States, and but a small portion of them actually joined the ranks of the army. This draft constituted the last demand of the general Government for men previous to the inauguration of the system of conscription in the following Spring "—(Report of Adjt.-Genl. Hillhouse, of New York). A law of the State of New York then in force required an enrolment of all persons liable to bear arms. No appropriation had been made by the Legislature for carrying the law into effect. The means were, however, provided on the personal responsibility of Governor Morgan, and an enrolment was made prior to the call of August 4, 1862. But as the enrolment was thought to be too imperfect for the draft ordered by the President, and as the War Department had issued instructions and provided means for an enrolment,* and had ordered that an allowance prior to draft be made to towns and counties for volunteers previously furnished, a new enrolment was ordered in New York. This was in the fall of 1862. It is mentioned to show, as explained by General Hillhouse, Adjutant-General of New York, in his report of December 31, 1862, that the United States enrolment made in 1863, which is especially discussed further on, was no strange measure to the people of New York, and that lack of ac-

---

* This, however, was not under the so-called enrolment act, which was not passed till March, 1863.

quaintance with the subject was not the reason why they at first failed to aid in making and correcting it.

Speaking of the State enrolment of 1862, General Hillhouse says : " In anticipation of a draft every citizen who was himself enrolled felt at once a personal interest in the completeness of the work, and instead of offering impediments to its prosecution, naturally desired that every person within the prescribed ages should be entered on the lists," and he adds that "the enrolment was entirely successful." But, as reported by General Hillhouse, although the draft for nine months' militia was for various reasons deferred, it had resulted in promoting enlistments and completing the quota under the call of July 2d, for volunteers for three years, and 30,000 three years' men in addition, to count against the last call, that of August 4, 1862. But nevertheless at the close of Governor Morgan's term, December 31, 1862, General Hillhouse reports the State as deficient 28,517 men in volunteers furnished since July 2, 1862, and of this deficiency he says 18,523 belonged to the *City of New York*. He, however, modifies the effect of this large proportion adverse to the City by saying, "It should be stated here that the credit to the City and County of New York is based on the actual returns filed in this office, but it is believed that it is less than the volunteers furnished."

In the State of New York an active and exciting political struggle took place in the autumn of 1862. General James S. Wadsworth, an eminent citizen and a distinguished officer of the Union Army, had been called from the field to run as the Republican candidate for Governor against Horatio Seymour, also an eminent and highly respected citizen, who was the candidate of the Democratic party.

Speaking in a political sense, rigorous prosecution of the war was a Republican measure ; and the opposition to the war was embodied in the Democratic party.   In New York the Democratic platform of 1862 was very brief.   It denounced arbitrary arrests, supported the use of " all legitimate means to suppress the rebellion and restore the Union as it was, and maintain the Constitution as it is ; " resolved, that " the war was not waged in any spirit of oppression or for any purpose of conquest or subjugation, or purpose of overthrowing or interfering with the rights or established institutions of those States, but to defend and maintain the supremacy of the Constitution, and to preserve the Union with all the dignity, equality, and rights of the several States unimpaired, and that as soon as these objects are accomplished the war ought to cease."

The Republican platform was elaborate and radical.   It urged the Government to prosecute the war by all the means " that the God of battles " had " placed in its power."   The confiscation of the property of "traitors in arms " was advocated, the President's intention to emancipate slaves was emphatically approved, and the enrolling, arming, and disciplining the militia of the States recommended.

The election resulted in favor of Seymour.   The first fourteen districts, which include Brooklyn and New York City (where the riots subsequently occurred), gave him a majority of 54,582 ; the remainder of the State gave Wadsworth a majority of 43,830, electing Seymour by a majority of 10,752.

On the 1st of January, 1863, the outgoing administration of Governor Morgan turned over to the incoming

administration of Governor Seymour, the revised State
enrolment, the Government's order for draft of the militia
and the deficiency of New York heretofore mentioned ;
and facts and details in connection with these matters as
well as with the general subject of recruitment, were spread
upon the records of the State by the comprehensive and
able report heretofore mentioned of Adjutant-General
Hillhouse. At this period the activity in the reinforcement of the armies which had marked the first year of the
war was replaced by industry and ingenuity in the preparation of "claims" by the various States, counties, and
towns, for men previously furnished. It is due to New
York to say that under the readjustment arising from these
"claims" for credit, it was conceded in the summer of
1863 that she had a small surplus instead of a deficiency.
But volunteering was practically at an end as a system in
itself to be relied upon for strengthening the army.

"The desire to enter the service, prompted by the first
ebullition of military ardor, had subsided and was replaced
by the popular demand that the different States should
furnish proportional numbers of men for the army."

"The demand for reinforcements from the various
armies in the field steadily and largely exceeded the cur-
rent supply of men. The old agencies for filling the ranks
proved more and more ineffective. It was evident that
the efforts of the Government for the suppression of the
rebellion would fail without resort to the unpopular but,
nevertheless, truly republican measure of conscription.
The national authorities, no less than the purest and wis-
est minds in Congress, and intelligent and patriotic citizens throughout the country, perceived that besides a more
reliable, regular, and abundant supply of men, other sub-
stantial benefits would be derived from the adoption and

enforcement of the principle that every citizen owes military service to the country in the hour of extremity. It would effectually do away with the unjust and burdensome disproportion in the number of men furnished by different States and localities." (Report of P. M. G.).

In a letter dated August 4, 1862, to Count A. de Gasparin, President Lincoln said: "Our great army has dwindled rapidly, bringing the necessity for a new call earlier than was anticipated. We shall easily obtain the new levy, however. Be not alarmed if you shall learn that we have resorted to a draft for part of this. It seems strange even to me, but it is true, that the Government is now pressed to this course by a popular demand. Thousands who wish not to personally enter the service are nevertheless anxious to pay and send substitutes, provided they can have assurance that unwilling persons similarly situated will be compelled to do likewise."

Henry Wilson (Republican) said in the Senate: "The immense numbers already summoned to the field, the scarcity and high rewards of labor, press upon all of us the conviction that the ranks of our wasted regiments cannot be filled again by the old system of volunteering. The needs of the nation demand that we should rely not upon volunteering, nor upon the calling forth of the militia, but that we should fill the regiments now in the field, worn and wasted by disease and death, by enrolling and drafting the population of the country under the constitutional authority to raise and support armies."

Senator Richardson (Democrat) said: "I agree with the Senator from Massachusetts that it is necessary to fill up the ranks of our army; and that it is necessary there should be a conscription bill."

Senator McDougal (Democrat) said: "Now in regard

to the conscription question I will say for myself that I regretted much, when this war was first organized, that the conscription rule did not obtain. I went from the extreme east to the extreme west, of the loyal States. I found some districts where some bold leaders brought out all the young men, and sent them or led them to the field. In other districts, and they were the most numerous, the people made no movement towards the maintenance of the war; there were whole towns and cities I may say, where no one volunteered to shoulder a musket, and no one offered to lead them into the service. The whole business has been unequal and wrong from the first. The rule of conscription should have been the rule to bring out men of all classes, and make it equal throughout the country, and therein the North has failed."

These are merely brief examples of the opinions and sentiments which resulted in the passage of the Act of March 3, 1863, entitled " *An Act* for enrolling and calling out the national forces and for other purposes." The main requirements of the law were the enrolment and draft of the national forces and the arrest of deserters. In his final report, dated March 17, 1866, the Provost Marshal General said : " The public safety would have been risked by longer delay in the enactment of this law. A general apathy prevailed throughout the country on the subject of volunteering. Recruiting had subsided, while desertion had greatly increased, and had grown into a formidable and widespread evil. The result of the important military operations during the first months of 1863 had been unfavorable and exercised a depressing effect upon the public mind. The battle of Stone River left the Army of the Cumberland crippled upon the field, and forced it to inactivity for months in an intrenched camp.

Our advance on Vicksburg by way of Haines' Bluff had been repulsed with serious loss. A knowledge of the extent of the disaster at Fredericksburg had reached and dispirited the loyal people. The first attack on Fort Sumter by the Navy had failed. The short but bloody and disastrous campaign of Chancellorsville was made, and the Army of the Potomac once more confined to the defensive. The rebel army was stronger in numbers than at any other period of the war. And last, not least, a powerful party in the North, encouraged by these events, opposed the raising of the new levies, and especially the enforcement of the new conscription law." It was a palpable fact at the period referred to, that our success depended on raising more troops, and that more troops could be raised only by carrying out the enrolment act. Defeat of the enforcement of this measure would have been the loss of the Union cause.

Affairs had reached such a point in the spring of 1863 that, for high public officers at least, there was no neutral ground between supporting the enforcement of the Enrolment Act and the prosecution of the war as part and parcel of the same thing, and opposing them. A Governor who was not unmistakably for them was, under the attending circumstances, by the very nature of his position, *against* them. Horatio Seymour was then Governor of the State of New York. He thought conscription unwise.

The only officers authorized by the Enrolment Act were a Provost Marshal General of the United States, and a Provost Marshal for each Congressional District. For the purposes of enrolment and draft a board was created in each district consisting of the Provost Marshal, a so-called Commissioner, and a Surgeon. This board had power to appoint persons to make the enrolment. The criticisms

of the enrolment and draft in certain districts of New
York City, make it necessary to explain who were appointed to office under the Enrolment Act for those districts, and upon what recommendations the appointees
were chosen.

The Provost Marshals were :

4th District.—Joel B. Erhardt (recommended by F. A.
Conkling, Mayor Opdyke, Henry J. Raymond, L. E.
Chittenden, E. C. Benedict, E. Delafield Smith, Wm.
M. Evarts, Wm. Hunt, General John P. Hatch and
others).

5th District.—John Duffy (recommended by Horace
Greeley, Wm. Hall, Judges Hilton, Daly and White,
Mayor Opdyke, H. J. Raymond, W. C. Bryant, Jas.
T. Brady and Edwards Pierrepont).

6th District.—James W. Farr (recommended by Governor Morgan and F. A. Conkling).

7th District.—Frederick C. Wagner (recommended by
Governor Morgan, Senator Harris, Mayor Opdyke,
and Thurlow Weed).

8th District.—Benj. F. Manierre (recommended by
Preston King, Horace Greeley, Hiram Barney, Wm.
C. Bryant, Curtis Noyes, and Geo. P. Putnam.

9th District.—Chas. E. Jenkins (recommended by
Mayor Opdyke, Edgar Ketchum, D. Dudley Field,
Edwards Pierrepont, and Hiram Walbridge).

The recommendations on which Commissioners and
Surgeons were appointed were generally the same and
in all cases as good as those for the Provost Marshals.
The foregoing specification of indorsers and the remarks
which follow concerning the officers detailed as Provost

Marshals General of the State of New York are given as
bearing on the charges of injustice, outrage, etc., made
concerning the enrolments and draft in the districts pre-
sided over by the gentlemen named. Although these
men, residents of New York City, were officers of the
general Government, proceeding under an act of Congress,
the War Department was alive to the necessity of securing the co-operation of State authorities in administering
the enrolment act, and, knowing that it would not be
practicable for the Provost Marshal General in Washington to gather detailed reports from every district in the
United States, cull them, and then supply the Governors
of States with all the particulars which it might be well
for them to have, nor convenient to Governors to depend on such a resource, resolved to place an officer of
the army on duty at the capital of each State to act as
Provost Marshal General for the State. Instead, however, of having but one such officer in New York, it was
thought best to place three in that State, making for that
purpose the northern, southern, and western divisions.
In selecting officers to occupy these positions care was
taken to seek those who would be likely to secure the
favor and co-operation of the authorities and the people
of New York. Major Fred. Townsend, 18th U. S. Infantry, was, on the 25th of April, 1863, detailed for the
northern division, Headquarters at Albany. Major (now
General) Townsend was a well-known and highly esteemed
resident of Albany, who held the office of Adjutant-
General of the State prior to the war, and has held the
same office since.

Colonel Robert Nugent, 69th New York Volunteers,
an honorable man, a gallant officer, a *war-democrat*, an
Irishman, a resident of New York City, was assigned to

the southern division, embracing New York City and Brooklyn; and for the western division, Major A. S. Diven, of the 107th Regiment New York Volunteers, was designated May 15th. He was a resident of Elmira, of superior ability and unimpeachable character, a *war-demo-crat*, and, as stated by Mr. W. H. Seward,—at whose instance he was selected,—an intimate acquaintance and personal friend of Governor Seymour.

These are the gentlemen under whom the United States enrolment and draft of 1863 were conducted.

But the efforts of the War Department to acquaint the Governor with all that was going on under the enrolment act, and secure his co-operation did not end with the mere assignment to duty of the three officers just named. On the dates mentioned above as those of their assignment, a formal letter of instructions* was given each of the three, from which the following is an extract:

"While the Governor of New York has no control over you, you will be required to acquaint yourself with his views and wishes and give them due weight in determining as to the best interests of the general Government, of which you are the representative. To this end you will use all proper means to gain and to retain the confidence and good-will of the Governor and his State officers. You will endeavor by all means in your power to secure for the execution of the Enrolment Act, the aid and hearty co-operation of his Excellency the Governor, and of the civil officers in his State, as also of the people."

A letter in terms as follows was addressed to Governor Seymour (and similar letters to other Governors):

---

* See Appendix B.

"Provost Marshal General's Office, }
Washington, D. C., *April* 24, 1863. }

"*To His Excellency Horatio Seymour,*
Governor of New York.

"Sir: With a view to uniform and harmonious execution of the Enrolment Act it has been deemed best to assign an officer of this Department of rank to duty at the Capital of New York. He will be instructed to confer with your Excellency, to superintend the operations of the Provost Marshals and Boards of Enrolment in the several Districts of the State, excepting the first nine, to secure from the Provost Marshals and Boards and submit to the State Executive such rolls and reports as may be deemed necessary for the files of the State, and to prepare from the State records, and transmit to the Provost Marshals and Boards of Enrolment such information placed at his disposal by the State authorities as may be necessary or useful to them in the performance of the duties assigned them. With similar views and for a like purpose it has been decided to assign an officer to the City of New York to exercise the same functions for the first nine Congressional Districts of your State.

" In accordance with the foregoing, Major Frederick Townsend, 18th U. S. Infantry, has been directed to take post at Albany, and Col. Robert Nugent, 69th N. Y. Vols., at New York City.

" These are officers of superior ability and gentlemen of attainments, and it is hoped their assignment will prove agreeable to your Excellency.

" The War Department will be pleased if your Excellency will communicate freely with them and secure, as far as possible, for all officers appointed under the Enrolment Act, the co-operation of the civil officers of your State.

" I am, Sir,

" Very respectfully

" Your obedient Servant,

(*Signed*)   " JAMES B. FRY.

" *Pro.-M'l. General.*"

A similar letter * was addressed to the Mayor of New York City, on whom Colonel Nugent called for co-operation as he did on the Governor.

The foregoing arrangements made by the War Department, enabled Governors to keep themselves as fully informed as they chose to be concerning the enrolment and draft in their respective States, and with very few exceptions, harmony and co-operation between the States and the United States were secured. It will be seen further on, however, that when the draft was ordered in July, 1863, that fact was made known to the Governor of New York and other Governors by *special* letters.

Presuming that military guards for the Provost Marshals in the City of New York would be necessary, a letter on that subject was addressed to General Wool, May 21, 1863, by the Provost Marshal General, in which he said:

" I have the honor to request that you will give the requisite orders to furnish the Provost Marshals of the different districts in the City of New York with such guards as may be necessary at their respective Headquarters until their places can be supplied by men from the Invalid Corps, now organizing.

---

* See Appendix C.

3

" Col. Robert Nugent, A. A. P. M. Gen'l for New York
City, is directed to call upon you and confer in regard
to this matter."

THE ENROLMENT.

Under these preliminary arrangements, the enrolment
of 1863 began.

It was of great importance to the people of the State as
well as to the general Government that a correct enrolment should be made. The Adjutant-General of New
York, when speaking, in his report of December 31, 1862,
of the principle of compulsory service, said to the Governor : " Nor is it less a matter of interest to the States.
Whatever may be the plan adopted, the force required
must be drawn from their population liable to military
duty, on which the 1,000,000 of volunteers hitherto sent to
the field has already made serious inroads. They have,
moreover, a common interest with the general Government in such an application of their military resources as
will render them most effective for the purposes in view
with the least possible waste, and with as little hardship
as possible to the community."

The co-operation of the State authorities so plainly
pointed out in the foregoing quotation as essential to the
welfare of the State, and which was so earnestly solicited
by the War Department, was almost indispensable to a
correct enrolment and a just apportionment of compulsory
service. But Governor Seymour gave no assistance ; in
fact, so far as the Government officers engaged in the enrolment could learn, he gave the subject no attention. But
he subsequently urged that the draft should be abandoned
on account of errors, which he alleged, in the enrolment,
and which, if they existed, he had failed to co-operate in

preventing. Documents hereinafter cited will define more plainly his position in the matter.

The Enrolment Act was approved March 3, 1863. Section 9 required that the enrollers " *immediately* proceed to enrol " and report the result " on or before the 1st day of April " to the Board of Enrolment, and the Board was required by the Act to consolidate the names into one list and transmit the same to the Provost Marshal General " on or before the 1st day of May." There was, it is true, a proviso that if these duties *could not* be done in the time specified, they should be performed as soon thereafter as practicable; but neither the intention of the law, nor the manifest necessity under which it was enacted, permitted delay, or, as President Lincoln expressed it in his letter to Governor Seymour, dated August 7, 1863, " we could not waste time to re-experiment with the volunteer system already deemed by Congress, and palpably in fact, so far exhausted as to be inadequate; and then more time to obtain a correct decision as to whether a law is constitutional which requires a part of those not now in the service to go to the aid of those who are already in it ; and still more time to determine with absolute certainty that we get those who are to go in the precisely legal proportion to those who are not to go." " My purpose," the President added, " is to be in my actions just and constitutional, and yet practical in performing the important duty with which I am charged, of maintaining the unity and the free principles of our common country."

This is enough to indicate the extreme pressure under which the enrolment was made in the spring of 1863. The co-operation of the State authorities was earnestly sought, the enrollers were carefully selected by the Boards composed of well selected citizens, and were sworn to execute faithfully and without partiality or favor the duties of their offices, and commenced their labors about the 25th of May.

The manner of making this enrolment and some particulars in relation to it are shown in Appendix D.

THE DRAFT.

The law made it the duty of the President to draft into the army as many of the men liable to service, borne on the enrolment, as he might from time to time find necessary, coupled with the condition, however, that in assigning quotas the number of volunteers and militia, and the periods of their service, previously furnished by the several States, should be duly credited.

That there might be no loss of time, as soon as the enrolment of a district was completed, the President made an order on that district for one-fifth of its enrolled men of the class liable to be called out.

The first order for draft, under the Enrolment Act, in the State of New York was issued July 1, 1863, for the 30th District. Orders immediately followed for drafts in other districts, some of them being in the City of New York.

Colonel Nugent, Assistant Provost Marshal General of Southern New York, was told in a letter of July 7th from the Provost Marshal General, " Should you consider it most expedient to do so, you are at liberty to execute the draft in New York City by districts, in one or more at a given time, rather than simultaneously throughout the city." He began on Saturday, July 11. The following account, from Appleton's *Encyclopaedia*, of what occurred, is substantially confirmed by the official records and is sufficiently accurate :

The Riot.—" The several deputies received official requisitions direct from the President, calling for specified numbers of men, and were instructed to commence operations on the 11th of July. In compliance with this order Provost Marshal Jenkins, of the ninth congressional district in New York, publicly announced through the press, that on Saturday, the 11th, the ballots would be publicly counted at the corner of Forty-sixth Street and Third Avenue, and that immediately thereafter the wheel would be turned and the draft begin. Rumors of popular dissatisfaction were heard on every side, trouble was apprehended, and the police were notified to hold themselves in readiness for any emergency. On Saturday morning a large crowd assembled at the appointed place, but as everything was conducted quietly, systematically, and fairly, no opportunity for disturbance occurred. The day passed pleasantly, the crowd were in good humor, well-known names were saluted with cheers, and at night, as the superintendent of the police passed out from the office, he remarked that there was no danger to be apprehended ; the Rubicon was passed, and all would go well. The names of the conscripts were published by the press of Sunday morning, with incidents, jocular and otherwise, connected with the proceedings. In the neighborhood in which the initial working of the law was attempted, an excitable element of the city's population resided. Very many poor men were, by the turn of the wheel, forced instantly, as it were, from home and comfort, wrested from the support of a needy family, to be sent they knew not whither, perhaps to the battle field, or, perhaps, to the grave. Such were the apprehensions of many imprudent persons, who were liable to the draft, and such their anxieties for the fate of their wives and children, that associations were formed to resist it, at the last alternative, with bloodshed." * * *

It is not necessary to go into the details of the riot, which continued for four days. The main purpose is in consequence of the articles cited in the beginning to show the attitude of Governor Seymour towards the Enrolment Act and the riot. Those articles give it as a positive and important assertion from him that he was not notified of the draft, the implication being that the Government authorities had in this respect, through design or neglect, omitted an important act of courtesy or duty; and that if the Governor had been notified he could and would have done something to prevent the riot or would have made preparations to suppress it. There is nothing in the history of the affair to encourage the belief that if the Governor had regarded the notices which were sent to him, he would have done anything else than strive to have the draft abandoned or postponed. But to leave the field of conjecture, the fact is that the Governor was formally and distinctly notified of the draft. By the following letters the Provost Marshal General not only notified him, but closed the notification by saying: " I beg that you will do all in your power to enable the officers acting under me to complete the draft, promptly, effectually, fairly and successfully."

"PROVOST MARSHAL GENERAL'S OFFICE,
WASHINGTON, D. C., *July* 1, 1863.

" *His Excellency, Horatio Seymour,*
Governor of New York, Albany, N. Y.

" SIR:—Orders have this day been sent to the Board of Enrolment in the 30th District of New York to make a draft in that District for 2539 men of the first class.

It is deemed important not to invite public discussion as to operations under the Enrolment Act, but it is proper that I should advise you of such steps taken under it as may bear upon your State.

" The records from which calculations were made as well as the calculations themselves determining the quota are on file in this office; they are impartial and claimed to be entirely correct, but if an error should be discovered or pointed out in them it will be duly corrected in the next subsequent draft.

" I beg that you will do all in your power to enable the officers acting under me to complete the draft promptly, effectually, fairly, and successfully.

" I am, Sir, Very Respectfully,
" Your Obedient Servant,
[*Signed.*]   " JAMES B. FRY,
" *Provost Marshal General.*"

A letter the same in terms as the foregoing but announcing the draft in the 8th district and also in the 15th, 21st, 26th, 28th and 29th, was sent to Governor Seymour by the Provost Marshal General on the 3d of July, 1863, and similar letters were sent as follows:

July, 6, 1863.   As to the 1st, 7th, 9th, 16th, and 25th Districts.

July 10, 1863.   As to the 10th District.

July 13, 1863.   As to the 2d, 13th, 23d, and 24th Districts.

July 24, 1863.   As to the 28th District.

July 28, 1863.   As to the 31st District.

The draft was commenced in the New England States before it was in New York. The arrangements for

furnishing the Governors of those States with information and the special notices of the draft sent to them (as
well in fact as to the Governors of all the States) corre-
sponded with those sent to the Governor of New York.
They made no complaint of lack of information.

Not only were the foregoing notifications sent to the
Governor of New York, but the following letter from him
is very good evidence that it was upon ample information
concerning the draft, if not upon these notifications that
he acted in sending his Adjutant-General to Washington
on the 11th of July, the very day the draft began in the
city, and two days before the riots, "*for the purpose of
urging a suspension of the draft.*"

New York, *July* 13, 1863.

"My Dear Sir:—I have received your note about
the draft. On Saturday last I sent my Adjutant-General
to Washington for the purpose of urging a suspension of
the draft, for I know that the City of New York can
furnish its full quota by volunteering. I have received a
despatch from General Sprague that the draft is suspended. There is no doubt the conscription is postponed. I learn this from a number of sources. If I get
any information of a change of policy at Washington I
will let you know.

"Truly Yours,
[*Signed.*] "Horatio Seymour.

" Hon. Samuel Sloan,
"President Hudson R. R. Co.,
"New York."

It seems therefore that the Governor had enough information about the draft to try to stop it.

These documents refute, in fact flatly contradict, the assertion in its broad meaning that the Governor was not notified of'the draft. But Governor Seymour is a man of strict integrity and great purity of character. There has probably been some misunderstanding as to his meaning if he denied that he was notified of the intended draft. The matter, therefore, requires more careful examination. Let us see exactly what was said. In his letter of August 3, 1863, to the President, the Governor stated in relation to the draft (which preceded the riot), " the Provost Marshal commenced this draft without consultation with the authorities of the State or of the city." In response to this the Provost Marshal General in a report to the Secretary of War, dated August 10, 1863, said, " Governor Seymour, who had been requested by my letter of 25th April to co-operate in carrying out the law, was, on the 1st of July, informed by my letter that the draft was ordered in the districts named, and was requested to aid in securing the execution of the orders. He has subsequently been duly informed of all orders issued for draft in the different districts of his State and his assistance solicited." Thus was this charge made and met officially in 1863. It, however, reappears formally, but not officially, these many years afterward. The *New York Herald* of November 4, 1878, quotes Governor Seymour as saying, " The riot was caused not only by an unjust enrolment, but by the way the draft was made. It was begun without giving any notice to * * * the Governor of the State ; " and the *New York Times* of August 28, 1879, and the book called *Twelve Americans*, say, it is presumed by the Governor's authority, " Governor Seymour never received any official notification that the draft was to commence or that it had com-

4

menced," and they add, the Provost Marshals, or those behind them, " threw prudence, propriety and common sense to the winds." Probably everybody who has read these articles has given them the meaning heretofore mentioned, to wit : that, in ordering the draft, the Government officers, through design or neglect, omitted an important act of courtesy or duty towards the State authorities, and that the latter were therefore absolved from responsibility for mischief which they might have prevented or mitigated if it had not been for the omission. The truth is, the Governor knew, and admitted at the time, that he had been notified of the draft.

In a letter to the President, dated August 21, 1863, he said (modifying the statement in his letter of August 3d), " in no instance have I received notice of the time when a draft was to be made in any district. The notices sent to me only stated that the enrolments were completed in certain districts, and that orders had been made directing a draft for the number to be taken from such districts. On Tuesday, the day before the draft was to be made in New York, I received a notice of this description, and this is the only official notice I have received with regard to it. These notices do not give any intimations when the draft will commence."

This letter shows that by August 21 the Governor's complaint that he had not been notified of the draft had assumed a much milder form, to wit: that he had not been notified of the exact time when the drawing of names from the wheel would begin. He admitted that he had been informed when the draft was ordered. The records confirm his admission, and show not only that he had been precisely and officially notified that the draft was ordered, but also that his co-operation in executing the law was solicited. The draft was ordered from Washington as soon as the Provost Marshal of a congressional district reported that he was ready; and the drawing of names by the Provost Marshal was commenced as soon as practicable after he received the order from Washington to proceed. As Governor Seymour was, in case of every district, formally notified when the draft was ordered, and was requested to aid in its enforcement, the modified complaint that he was not told when the actual drawing of names would begin in each case is not worthy of serious consideration. The officers charged with the conscription designed to give, and did give, to the Governor all the information in the matter of the enrolment and draft in his State that he could need; and there was no neglect or omission on the part of the general Government to which his action or want of action concerning the draft and the draft riots is in the slightest degree fairly attributable.

Furthermore, the Governor's complaint that he was not notified when the drawing would begin, might have been very easily forestalled by the Governor himself. The arrangement, heretofore explained, under which Assistant Provost Marshals General were on duty in New York, enabled the Governor to obtain quite as early notice of the drawings and the exact time fixed for them as the authorities in Washington could receive. The Assistant Provost Marshals General of States had no right to prevent or postpone the draft. Their duty was to enforce it, and the correspondence and intercourse between them and Governors concerning these drawings would necessarily relate to the co-operation proposed by the latter in the execution of the law. The occupations of Governor Seymour permitted but little, if any, intimate intercourse between him and the Assistant Provost Marshals General with a view to enforcing the draft, and this may in some degree account for his lack of familiarity with operations which so urgently needed his aid and encouragement.

In the newspaper articles and the book already cited— if he is correctly quoted in them—as well as in his letter of August 3, 1863, to the President, the Governor speaks disapprovingly of the fact that the draft was ordered while much of the available militia of the State was absent, aiding to repel the rebel invasion of Pennslyvania. It must be remembered that the same invasion which called away the militia impressed on the Government the necessity for *immediate* enforcement of the draft, to strengthen the army.

It was somewhat unfortunate that while the militia was absent, and when the draft about which the Governor felt so much apprehension, which was in progress in New England, with the noise of which the whole country was ringing, and which Governor Seymour had been formally notified was to be commenced in New York City, both the Governor and his Adjutant-General—as well as the militia—should be absent from the State, the former at Long Branch, and the latter in Washington, by the former's orders, trying to prevent the draft in New York.*

Fortunately the invaders of Pennsylvania were beaten back. The campaign of Gettysburg ended in our favor,

---

* The *New York Times* says that when Governor Seymour heard at Long Branch of the disturbances in New York City, "he hurried to the metropolis without having tasted food." Why the Governor fasted at Long Branch is a mystery.

and part of the Army of the Potomac became available for the campaign in New York.

But if the militia had been at home, would the Governor have marshaled his forces on the assumption that the people of New York City were going to resort to a formidable violation of law and order ? Would he have agreed that the President should concentrate Federal forces in New York on such an assumption ? The argument in relation to such proceedings would have been that a threat of that kind was an insult to the good citizens of New York, and was likely to create the resistance and violence which the display of military force was intended to prevent.

The question is, was it, under the circumstances, throwing "prudence, propriety, and common sense to the winds" to begin the draft in New York City with such preparations only as were actually made ? If so, what *ought* to have been done ? It must be conceded that the Enrolment Act was passed to be promptly enforced. There was no dispute that a pressing necessity existed for more troops. The enforcement of the law was the way provided by Congress—if it was not the only way—to obtain them. The draft was going on favorably in New England. It was about to be started in various parts of the country. The Provost Marshals in charge of districts in New York City had reported the completion of the enrolment and readiness for the draft. The Governor of New York had been requested to co-operate, and up to that time had made no objection and given no warning of danger. The questions were, should the draft go on in New York City, as elsewhere, should it be abandoned or postponed there, or should resistance be assumed and military force presumably large enough to overawe or overcome a formidable uprising be concentrated in the city before trying to execute the law without such threatening preparations? These questions were carefully weighed by the President and by the War Department. The conclusions were that no exception in the application of the law should be made in New York, that no presumption that the State or City authorities would fail to co-operate with the Government should be admitted, that a Federal military force ought not to be assembled in New York City on the mere assumption that a law of the United States would be violently and extensively resisted, and that if it were thought best to assemble such a force, there was none to be had without losing campaigns then going on, or battles then impending.

It was therefore resolved to proceed with the draft on the assumption that the law could be enforced without an army, to have the police on hand in full force at the places of draft, and small military guards in attendance at suitable points. In the light of over 22 years it has not been made to appear that more military preparations would have been justifiable under the circumstances, nor that the draft should have been abandoned or postponed.

Beginning the drawing on Saturday has been given as one of the causes of the riot, and that perhaps is what is referred to in speaking of the faulty manner of making the draft. It is true that as Sunday intervened between beginning and ending the drawing in the district where the riot began, a day was thus afforded for the operation of bad influences. But the same length of time was afforded for the operation of good influences, and perhaps it was admissible in this Christian land and in the loyal State of New York to hope for as much effect on Sunday from the latter as from the former. The criticism of beginning on Saturday seems rather trivial. Law-breakers do not regulate their depredations by the days of the week. But it must be acknowledged that what bad judgment there was in beginning the drawings on Saturday is chargeable to officers of the general Government who acted under the demand, which admitted of no delay, for recruits to strengthen the armies in the field.

In his letter of August 3d, 1863, to the President, Governor Seymour, said :

" As the draft was one of the causes of the late riot in the city of New York, and as that outbreak had been urged by some as a reason for its immediate execution in that city, it is proper that I should speak of that event. I know you will agree with me that justice and prudence alike demand that this lottery for life should be conducted with the utmost fairness and openness, so that all may know that it is impartial and equal in its operation. It is the right of every citizen to be assured that in all public transactions there is strict impartiality. In a matter so deeply affecting the persons and happiness of our people this is called for by every consideration. I am happy to say that in many of the districts in this State the enrolled lists were publicly exhibited, the names were placed in the wheels from which they were to be drawn in the presence of men of different parties and of known integrity, and the drawings were conducted in a manner to avoid suspicion of wrong. As the enrolments are made in many instances by persons unknown to the public, who are affected by their actions, and who have no voice in their selection, care should be taken to prove the correctness of every step. Unfortunately this was not

done in the district of New York where the drawing commenced. The excitement caused by this unexpected
draft, led to an unjustifiable attack upon the enrolling
officers, which ultimately grew into the most destructive
riot known in the history of our country."

As confirmatory of the Governor's purpose in this letter
to attribute the riots to the enrolment, in part at least,
the *Herald* article heretofore given quotes him as saying :
"The riot was caused not only *by an unjust enrolment*,
but by the way the draft was made." That is to say, the
Governor offers an alleged unfair enrolment and an "*unexpected*" draft as causes for the riot. The act of Congress was passed for the purpose of raising troops by
draft, and the enrolment was made with a view to that
operation. The President's orders required a draft ; these
orders were made known not only to the Provost Marshals, but to the Governors of States. The drawing was
commenced in Rhode Island, July 7th ; in Massachusetts,
July 8th. The newspapers of the day teemed with accounts of it. There was therefore no conceivable reason
why the draft which began in New York City July 11,
1863, should have been *unexpected*. Nor is there any
good ground for the intimation that the nature of the
enrolment had any influence in producing the riot. No
complaint of the enrolment was received by the War
Department from Governor Seymour or any one else until the riots had occurred, nor had any claim been made
that quotas should be calculated on population or any
other basis than the enrolment. It was entirely an after-
thought to depict the alleged over-enrolment in some of
the city districts as a wrong, and one of such elasticity
that it might be drawn back to serve as an explanation
of riotous crimes for which there was, even on the part

of the criminals themselves, no pretence that it had been the cause.*

The real cause of the riot was that in a community where a considerable political element was active in opposition to the way the war was conducted, if not to the war itself, and where there was a strong opinion adverse to the principles of compulsory service, certain lawless men pre ferred fighting the Government at home, when it made the issue of *forcing* them by lot to fight its enemies in the field.

Governor Seymour was one of those whose convictions were against the wisdom of trying to force men into the army, if not against the right of the Government to do so. His arguments and efforts were not aimed at an improvement in the processes for enrolment, but at preventing any draft at all. A few facts will serve to justify this statement. While the riot was going on he had an interview with Colonel Nugent, the acting Provost Marshal General, New York City, and insisted on the Colonel's announcing a suspension of the draft. The draft had already been stopped by violence. The announcement was urged by the Governor, no doubt, because he thought it would allay the excitement; but it was, under the circumstances, making a concession to the mob, and endangering the successful enforcement of the law of the land.

On the 19th of July the Governor addressed a letter as follows to the President :

" At my request the Honorable Samuel J. Tilden goes

---

* On the 16th of July the U. S. Marshal, Robert Murray, telegraphed the Secretary of War, " I have arrested the principal orator of the mob, a Southern man by the name of Andrews." There is nothing to show that this orator of the mob had charged the riot as due in any degree to the character of the enrolment, or the manner of making the draft.

5

to Washington for the purpose of stating to you my views
and wishes with regard to affairs in this State. He is
thoroughly acquainted with my opinions and purposes. I
trust you will give him an opportunity to communicate
with you at length. I shall also address a letter to you
in the course of a few days."

The connection between the visit and the draft is shown
by the first paragraph of the letter from the Governor,
heretofore mentioned. It was dated August 3d, and
began :

" At my request a number of persons have called upon
you with respect to the draft in this State, more particularly as it affected the cities of New York and Brooklyn." * * *

This letter of August 3d was preceded by a telegram
from the Governor to the President, saying : " I ask that
the draft be suspended in this State until I can send to
you a communication I am preparing." This was followed by another telegram dated August 3d, saying in
answer to an inquiry from the President, " My letter will
reach you on Wednesday. I wish all drafts delayed, particularly in New York and Brooklyn."

In his letter of August 3d the Governor says, " The harsh
measure of raising troops by compulsion has heretofore
been avoided by the Government. * * * I believe it
will be found that the abandonment of voluntary enlistments for a forced conscription will prove to be unfortunate as a policy. * * * I ask that the draft may be suspended in this State, as has been done elsewhere, until
we shall learn the results of recruiting, which is now
actively going on. It is believed by at least one-half of
the people of the loyal States that the Conscription Act,
which they are called upon to obey because it stands on

the statute book, is in itself a violation of the Supreme Constitutional law. * * * The successful execution of the conscription act depends upon the settlement by judicial tribunals of its constitutionality. * * * It should be determined in advance of the enforcement which must be destructive of so many lives. It would be cruel mockery to withhold such decision until after the irremediable injury of its execution. * * * I do not dwell upon what I believe would be the consequence of a violent, harsh policy, before the constitutionality of the act is tested. You can scan the immediate future as well as I. I earnestly request that you will direct that the enrolling officers shall submit to the State authorities their lists, and that an opportunity shall be given to me as Governor of this State, and to other proper State officials to look into the fairness of these proceedings."

To look into the fairness of the enrolment and contribute to it, was just what the Governor, without effect, had been earnestly requested to do by the Provost Marshal General's letter of April 25, 1863. His compliance would have contributed to a more prompt and equitable enforcement of the draft. To have submitted the lists to " the State authorities " in August, could have resulted only in defeating the draft, or at least leaving the time of its enforcement subject to the discretion of those who did not want it enforced at all.

This probably is enough to show that the Governor's hostility was to the measure itself rather than to the manner of its execution, but more conclusive proof is given in the appendix, documents E., F., G., H., I. and J. being letters from Generals Diven, Canby and Dix.

President Lincoln, fully comprehending that the Governor's object was defeat or postponement of the draft,

answered accordingly.   In a letter to the Governor, dated
August 7, 1863, after making an arbitrary reduction of the
quotas in certain districts in New York, the President
said :

"Your communication of the 3d instant has been received and attentively considered.   I cannot consent to
suspend the draft in New York, as you request, because
among other reasons time is too important.

    *   *   *   *   *   *

"I shall direct the draft to proceed in all the districts,
drawing, however, at first from each of the four districts,
to wit : the second, fourth, sixth and eighth, only two
thousand two hundred being the average quota of the
other class.   After this drawing, these four districts, and
also the seventeenth and twenty-ninth shall be carefully
re-enrolled and, if you please, agents of yours may witness
every step of the process.

    *   *   *   *   *   *

"I do not object to abide a decision of the United
States Supreme Court, or of the Judges thereof, on the
constitutionality of the draft law.   In fact, I would be
willing to facilitate the obtaining of it, but I can not consent to lose the time while it is being obtained."

    *   *   *   *   *   *

The foregoing letter from the President settled the question of delaying the draft on the ground of testing the
constitutionality of the law.   But by the time (August
8th) that decision reached the Governor he had received
from his Judge Advocate General, Nelson J. Waterbury,
a report on the subject of enrolment and draft, which enabled the Governor, in his future efforts to prevent a draft,
to give more prominence to alleged wrongs in the enrol-

ment. He wrote the President as follows on the 7th and 8th of August :

"ALBANY, *Friday, August* 7, 1863.

"*President of the United States,*

"DEAR SIR:—On Monday last, I sent you a communication with respect to the Conscription Act. I also sent some tables showing the injustice of the enrolment. To-morrow I will send you more full and accurate statements which will place the errors, if they are not shameless frauds, in a more clear and striking light. I think I have information as to the manner the law has been perverted which may enable Government to bring some of the enrolling officers to justice.

"However much I may differ from you in my views of the policy of your administration, and although I may, unconsciously to myself, be influenced by party prejudices, I can never forget the honor of my country so far as to spare any effort to stop proceedings under the draft in this State—and more particularly in the cties of New York and Brooklyn—which I feel will bring disgrace not only upon your administration, but upon the American name.

" I shall be able to send you those additional statements in the course of to-morrow.

"Truly Yours, etc.,

(*Signed*), " HORATIO SEYMOUR."

This letter was promptly supplemented as follows :

"ALBANY, *August* 8, 1863.

"*To the President of the United States.*

"DEAR SIR:—I received your communication of the 7th instant this morning. While I recognize the conces-

sions you have made, I regret your refusal to comply
with my request to have the draft in this State suspended
until it can be ascertained if the enrolments are made in
accordance with the laws of Congress or with principles
of justice. I know that our army needs recruits, and for
this among other reasons I regret a decision which
stands in the way of a prompt and cheerful movement
to fill up the thinned ranks of our regiments. New York
has never paused in its efforts to send volunteers to the
assistance of our gallant soldiers in the field. It has not
only met every call heretofore made, while every other
Atlantic and New England State save Rhode Island was
delinquent, but it continued liberal bounties to volunteers when all efforts were suspended in many other
quarters. Active exertions are now made to organize
new and fill up old regiments; these exertions would be
more succesful if the draft was suspended, and much
better men than reluctant conscripts would join our
armies.

" On the 7th inst. I advised you by letter that I would
furnish the strongest proofs of injustice, if not of fraud,
in the enrolments of certain districts. I now send you
a full report made to me by Judge Advocate General
Waterbury. I am confident when you have read it you
will agree with me that the honor of the nation and of
your administration demands that the abuses it points
out should be corrected and punished. You say that ' we
are contending with an enemy who as you understand
drives every able-bodied man he can reach into his ranks
very much as a butcher drives bullocks into a slaughter
pen.' You will agree with me that even this, if impar-
tially done to all classes, is more tolerable than any
scheme which shall fraudulently force a portion of the

community into military service by a dishonest perversion of the law. You will see by the report of Mr. Waterbury that there is no theory which can explain or justify the enrolments in this State. I wish to call your attention to the tables on pages five, six, seven and eight which show that in the nine congressional districts of Manhattan, Long and Staten Islands the number of conscripts called for is 33,729, while in nineteen other districts the number of conscripts called for is only 39,626! This draft is to be made upon the first class; upon those between the ages of twenty and thirty-five. It appears by the census of 1860 that in the first nine congressional districts there are 164,797 males between twenty and thirty-five. They are called upon for 33,729 conscripts. In the other nineteen districts, with a population of males between twenty and thirty-five of 270,786, only 39,626 conscripts are demanded. Again, to show the partisan character of the enrolment, you will find on the twentieth page of Mr. Waterbury's report that in the first nine congressional districts the total vote of 1860 was 151,243. The number of conscripts now demanded is 33,729. In the nineteen districts the total vote was 457,257, yet these districts are called upon to furnish only 39,626 drafted men. Each of the nine districts gave majorities in favor of one political party. Each of the nineteen districts gave majorities in favor of the other party. You can not and will not fail to right these gross wrongs.

" Truly Yours, etc.,
(*Signed.*) " HORATIO SEYMOUR."

In relation to the larger numbers of men found by the enrolment to be living in some districts than in others in

1863, it may be mentioned for what it is worth, that the war had then been going on about two years, and its early demands had skimmed off the cream of the nation's loyalty, and very naturally most men would be found remaining in those districts which were most unfriendly to the war or the manner in which the Government conducted it.

To the foregoing communications, the President, on the 11th of August replied as follows:

" EXECUTIVE MANSION, WASHINGTON, }
August 11, 1863. }

"His Excellency Horatio Seymour,
Governor of New York.

" Yours of the 8th instant with Judge Advocate General Waterbury's report was received to-day. Asking you to remember that I consider time as being very important both to the general cause of the country and to the soldiers already in the field, I beg to remind you that I waited at your request from the 1st to the 6th instant to receive your communication dated the 3rd. In view of its great length and the known time and apparent care in its preparation I did not doubt that it contained your full case as you desired to present it. It contained figures for twelve districts, omitting the other nineteen, as I supposed because you found nothing to complain of as to them. I answered accordingly. In doing so I laid down the principle to which I proposed adhering, which is to proceed with the draft, at the same time employing infallible means to avoid any great wrongs. With the communication received to-day you send figures for twenty-eight districts, including the twelve sent before, and still omitting three from which I suppose the enrolments are not yet received. In looking over the fuller list of twenty-eight districts, I find that the quotas for sixteen are above 2,000 and below 2,700, while of the rest six are above 2,700 and six are below 2,000. Applying the principle to these new facts, the 5th and 7th districts must be added to the four in which the quotas have already been reduced to 2,200 for the first draft and, with these four others, must be added to those to be re-enrolled. The corrected case will then stand : The quotas of the 2d, 4th, 5th, 6th, 7th, and 8th districts, fixed at 2,200 for the first draft. The Provost Marshal General informs me that the drawing is already completed in the 16th, 17th, 18th, 22d, 24th, 26th, 27th, 28th, 29th, and 30th districts. In the others, except the three outstanding, the drawing will be made upon the quotas now fixed. After the first draft the 2d, 4th, 5th, 6th, 7th, 8th, 16th, 17th, 21st, 25th, 29th, and 31st districts will be re-enrolled for the purpose and in the manner stated in my letter of the 7th instant. The same principle will be applied to the now outstanding districts when they shall come in.

"No part of my former letter is repudiated by reason of not being re-stated in this, or for any other cause.

" Your Obedient Servant,
(*Signed*)   "A. LINCOLN."

This practically terminated the controversy concerning the enrolment so far as the first draft (July, 1863) was concerned. The subject received further consideration, however, under a subsequent call for troops, as will be seen further on. A few words more are necessary to finish the account of the draft which had been stopped by the mob on the 13th of July, 1863.

In addition to other measures for suppressing the

6

riots, the Government promptly ordered home the New York militia, which had been sent to Pennsylvania, and on the 16th of July the Secretary of War telegraphed Governor Seymour as follows: "Eleven New York regiments are relieved and are at Frederick and will be forwarded to New York as fast as transportation can be furnished them. Please signify to me anything you may desire to be done by the Department. Whatever means are at its disposal shall be at your command for the purpose of restoring order in New York.

"EDWIN M. STANTON,
"*Secretary of War.*"

On the 17th of July the Provost Marshal General issued a circular in terms as follows:

"The operations of the draft lately ordered in the New England and Middle States, though in most instances completed or now in progress without opposition, have in one or two cities been temporarily interrupted. Provost Marshals are informed that no orders have been issued countermanding the draft. Adequate force has been ordered by the Government to the points where the proceedings have been interrupted. Provost Marshals will be sustained by the military forces of the country in enforcing the draft, in accordance with the laws of the United States, and will proceed to execute the orders heretofore given for draft as rapidly as shall be practicable by aid of the military forces ordered to co-operate with and protect them."

Prior to the resumption of the draft, General Dix was assigned to chief command in New York, with General Canby as immediate commander under him in the city. Letters from these two officers cited in another connection give some evidence of the necessity which had suddenly arisen for troops to carry out the laws. General Dix's efforts were directed first, but without success, to obtaining the requisite force from Governor Seymour, as shown by letter in Appendix K.

It was not until the 15th of August that the Governor answered General Dix's letters of July 30th and August 8th, asking that the State furnish the necessary force to execute the law. In consequence of the delay (see General Dix's letter, Appendix N.), Dix had already applied to the general Government for troops, which were sent.

The Governor said : " As you state in your letter that it is your duty to enforce the act of Congress, and as you apprehend its provisions may excite popular resistance, it is proposed you should know the position which will be held by the State authorities. Of course, under no circumstances can they perform duties expressly confided to others ; nor can they undertake to relieve others from their proper responsibilities. But there can be no violations of good order or riotous proceedings, no disturbances of the public peace which are not infractions of the laws of the State, and those laws will be enforced under all circumstances."

It will be observed that the only guarantee the Governor gave was that there should be no infractions of the *laws of the State*. He was asked whether he would aid in enforcing a law of the United States. As he gave no assurance on that point after the subject had undergone full discussion and the necessity for his co-operation had been demonstrated by the riots, it is not to be supposed that he would have aided in enforcing the obnoxious Conscription Act, even if he had known the very moment when the first name was to be drawn from the wheel by the

Provost Marshal at the corner of Forty-sixth Street and
Third avenue, where the riot began.

The Government had been forewarned by General Dix;
and telegrams, to be found in Appendices P. and Q., show
that military operations in Virginia were modified to
answer the public demands in New York, and give the
strength of the force detached from the Army of the Potomac to enforce the Enrolment Act in the Metropolis
of the Nation.

It was at that moment a fixed fact that the draft would
be made under the protection of the United States
forces; and that those forces would promptly and effectually put down any and all resistance. Then on the 18th
of August (1863) Governor Seymour issued a proclamation warning the people against disorders, and saying:
" I again repeat to you the warning which I gave to you
during the riotous proceedings of last month, that
the only opposition to the conscription which can be allowed is an appeal to the Courts." And adding: " I
hereby admonish all judicial and executive officers whose
duty it is to enforce the law and preserve public order,
that they take vigorous and effective measures to put
down any riotous or unlawful assemblages; and if they
find their power insufficient for that purpose, to call upon
the military in the manner pointed out by the Statutes
of the State. If these measures should prove insufficient, I shall then exert the full power of the State, in
order that the public order may be preserved, and the
persons and properties of the citizens be fully protected."

Owing to this proclamation, *and the presence of ten
thousand veteran troops from the Army of the Potomac,*
there was no resistance when the drawing was resumed

in New York City on the 19th of August (1863). The draft went on.

CLAIMS FOR CREDITS, &c.

The Enrolment Act required the President, in assigning quotas, to give credit for all volunteers and militia furnished from the beginning of the rebellion, and fairness, as well as the terms of the law, called for an adjustment of accounts. This brought about a general scramble for " credits," in which New York City came out eminently successful.

A large part of the energy and industry which characterized the raising of troops during the first two years of the war was, early in the third year, directed in the different States and districts to securing " credit " for what had been done, and reducing in due proportion the Government's demands for what remained to be done in the way of furnishing troops for the field. These credits were not only for the soldiers who actually took the field, but embraced that class referred to in the report of the Adjutant-General of New York of December 31, 1862, where he says, " the aggregate number of volunteers claimed to have been enlisted exceeds the number known to have left the State since July 2d, but the difference can readily be accounted for when it is considered that the offer of bounties by towns and counties has induced enlistments merely as a means of obtaining money. The desertions consequent on such a system and prompted by it, have reached an alarming extent and defied all ordinary means of prevention. It is believed that in the interior of the State the number of volunteers claimed is not in excess of the number actually enlisted, though in view of the fact that the payment of town bounties has induced desertion, and a large number of the recruits have been rejected on the final muster, it is no doubt in excess of the number that have actually entered the service. In the counties comprising the first seven districts, however, the difference between the number of volunteers claimed and the number known to have actually entered the service is so great as to render the reports from these districts unreliable as a basis for establishing their deficiencies. There is no doubt that the authorities have paid bounties to a large number of men who have subsequently deserted, and, indeed, who never had any intention of entering the service. So far from this, there is good evidence to believe that there has been an organized scheme through which large sums of money have been drawn from the authorities by persons who have at once disappeared, perhaps to repeat the operation in another locality. There is now at large in the districts mentioned a large number of persons who have deserted under these circumstances, and it is a question of importance to determine how far the counties are to have credit for them. It is claimed that the bounties have been paid in good faith and on evidence of enlistment and muster which appeared to justify it, and that having furnished the men and turned them over to the military authorities, the counties cannot thereafter be fairly held responsible for them, unless they were rejected on final muster. The answer to this is, that while the military authorities are responsible for desertions arising from ordinary causes, they cannot undertake to provide against it where the enlistment is part of a scheme to obtain money injudiciously offered after the liberal donations made by the State and general Government."

As early as August 21st, two days after the draft was

resumed in New York City, Governor Seymour sent a letter to the President urging the claims for " credits " of New York, especially the city, which was embraced in the districts above discussed by the Adjutant-General of the State. The President had the claims for " credits " adjusted as rapidly and as fairly as he could, but held to the enforcement of the Enrolment Act. His position on the subject is shown by the following telegram which he sent to Governor Seymour:

" Your dispatch of this morning is just received, and I fear I do not perfectly understand it. My view of the principle is that every soldier obtained voluntarily leaves one less to be obtained by draft. The only difficulty is in applying the principle properly. Looking to time, as heretofore, I am unwilling to give up a drafted man now even for the certainty, much less for the mere chance of getting a volunteer hereafter. Again, after the draft in any district, would it not make trouble to take a drafted man out and put a volunteer in, for how shall it be determined which drafted man is to have the privilege of thus going out to the exclusion of all the others? And even before the draft in any district the quota must be fixed ; and the draft might be postponed indefinitely if every time a volunteer is offered the officers must stop and reconstruct the quota. At least I fear there might be this difficulty ; but at all events let credit for volunteers be given up to the last moment which will not produce confusion or delay. That the principle of giving credit for volunteers shall be applied by districts seems fair and proper, though I do not know how far by present statistics it is practicable. When for any cause a fair credit is not given at one time, it should be given as soon thereafter as practicable.

My purpose is to be just and fair and yet not to lose
time.

"A. LINCOLN."

The letter of August 21st from Governor Seymour to
the President, mentioned above, also conveyed a statement
that residents of New York were being taken in great
numbers and enlisted in other States, and a request that
" a general order be published whereby all persons entering the military service of the United States as substitutes
for conscripts or otherwise shall be credited by the proper
authorities to the State in which they shall have been enrolled and liable to military service, and that such persons
be counted on the quota of such States." This, besides
raising a point of law, suggested delay, or as Mr. Lincoln
expressed it to Governor Seymour, it brought in *the element of time.* For example, if a man enrolled and liable
to duty in Connecticut were drafted, having by law the
privilege of going in person or furnishing a substitute, he
might present as his substitute a man from New York.
Under the proposed order the drafting officers would have
to ascertain the place of enrolment, etc., of the substitute,
and take the necessary steps for having him credited to
that place, which, of course, might be very remote, and
involve time and correspondence. But it also involved
charging to the account of the Government two soldiers
when it only got one. The legal point was referred to
the Judge Advocate General and he gave (See Appendix
R.) an opinion adverse to Governor Seymour.

SECOND CALL FOR TROOPS UNDER THE ENROLMENT ACT.

On the 17th of October, 1863, the President called for
300,000 volunteers, and ordered that a draft be made for

all deficiencies which might exist, January 5, 1864, on
the quotas assigned to districts by the War Department.
This brought up again the question of the enrolment in
New York. The *Herald* article heretofore embodied
quotes Governor Seymour as saying of the enrolment,
" the matter was the subject of a correspondence with
President Lincoln which resulted in the appointment by
the President of two men, and of one man by myself as
Governor, to conduct an inquiry. The two commissioners
named by the President were from other States, were officers of the army, and were naturally inclined to distrust
the charge of unfairness. They spent a long time in laborious research into the facts. Rising above all prejudice,
they decided that the quotas of New York and Brooklyn
were erroneous and excessive, and should be reduced."

The members of this commission were Wm. F. Allen,
of New York, John Love, of Indiana, and Chauncey Smith,
of Massachusetts. It is not correct, as stated above, that
two of them were officers of the army. Judge Allen, the
senior member, a man of unquestionable ability and integrity, was a prominent Democrat in politics. He was
selected by Governor Seymour. General Love had been
a Lieutenant in the army, but resigned February 1, 1853.
During the rebellion he was a "war" Democrat, and was
an active and influential member of the Democratic party
to the time of his death a few years ago. Mr. Smith, a
lawyer by profession, never an officer of the army, was
probably not specially attached to either political party.
These gentlemen acquitted the enrolling officers of the
charges of unfairness, outrage, grievous wrong-doing, etc.,
etc., which Governor Seymour brought at the time, and
which are repeated in the newspaper articles of 1878 and
1879 heretofore quoted, and in the book of 1883.

7

The Commission said: "Justice to the enrolling officers and agents requires that it should be distinctly stated
that their fidelity or integrity is by no means impeached
by any inaccuracies that may have existed in the enrolment. They were the necessary result of the execution
of the law under the circumstances, and with the means
at the command of the officers, and it is not perceived how
they could be avoided." In relation to the correction of
the enrolment, so as to make it a just and proper basis
for the assignment of quotas, the Commission said: "A
new enrolment was of course out of the question, and
could one have been made it is not perceived how the difficulties before encountered could have been overcome, or
the mistakes and errors of the first enrolment amended.
The same causes of error and imperfection still exist and
are at work, and would undoubtedly produce the same
results. The difficulty in the first enrolment was not in
the enrolling agents but in the system, and means and
appliances at the command of the agents. The Commission were unable to devise any process or means to correct
the enrolment and make it what it should be as a reliable
and satisfactory basis for the adjustment of quotas, * * *
and the Commission are of the opinion that any enrolment
made by faithful agents with the present limitations on
their powers and discretion, and with their present helps
and means, must be excessive and cannot constitute a
proper basis for apportionment of men to be furnished
upon a call for volunteers."

The Commission reached the conclusion that the "way
the error could be corrected and the quota made right"
was to adjust the quota "upon the basis and in proportion
to the entire population." This, the Commission thought,
would be constitutional and legal. On this point the

Commission added : " Without questioning or calling in question the construction of the Conscription Act in the orders or calls made under it, the Commission, in view of the fact that the enrolment is clearly and confessedly inaccurate and imperfect, and in the City of New York excessive, are unanimously of the opinion that the population constitutes the only safe and proper basis for the assignment of quotas and the apportionment of men to be furnished by the State of New York upon a call for volunteers. But while no other basis than the enrolment is recommended for any draft that may be ordered, the Commission are unanimously of the opinion and recommend that in any case if a State or district will and does furnish its just share and proportion of men required under any call or order for a draft, in proportion to population, such State or district should be held to have fully complied with the call and be relieved from the draft."

The conclusion of the Commission that population should be the basis for quotas, rests, mainly, on the assumption that (as they express it) " a call for volunteers is in one sense a tax upon the States and communities * * * so that the burthen falls upon property as directly as if Congress had laid a direct tax for the same purpose." The Commission held therefore that this process would be constitutional, and that it would be legal, they maintained because, as they reported, " in all the acts of Congress thus far passed upon the subject of raising volunteers by calls upon the several States, population has been made the basis of the apportionment. Acts of July 22, 1861, July 25, 1861, and July 17, 1862, are explicit upon the subject. These acts are not repealed and still apply to any calls made under them, and whether they should govern the call of October 17, 1863, is not for the Commission to decide. They are only referred to as expressions of the judgment of the legislature, of the proper basis for a call for volunteers, where no other mode is prescribed."

As soon as the Commission's report reached Washington the Provost Marshal General was required to give his views upon it, which he did both verbally and in writing. He pointed out the fact that the call of October 17, 1863, then pending, was not made under the Acts of 1861, or 1862, authorizing volunteers to be called out on the basis of population, but was made under the Enrolment Act of March 3, 1863, which called—as shown by the President's proclamation and instructions given at the time—for personal service and not taxes, and which required the apportionment of quotas to be made on the basis of the enrolment, and said: " The Commission has evidently been absorbed by the conviction that the raising of men is, and will necessarily continue, to be equivalent to levying special taxes and raising money, and they would therefore require the same proceeds under the Enrolment Act from a district of rich women which they would from a district with the same number of men of equal means. I assume that we are looking for personal military service from those able to perform it, that we make no calls for volunteers in the sense in which the Commission understands it, but that we assign to the districts under the Enrolment Act fair quotas of *the men* we have found them to contain." * * * " That for the Government to defer personal service for the purpose of enabling the people to raise money to be used as bounties would be to depart from the sound principles of the law by which it can require and secure the services of its forces."

The Provost Marshal General maintained that the Com-

mission were too strict and absolute in their construction
of the terms " erroneous and imperfect," as applied to
the enrolment, and of the term "just and equitable," as
applied to the quotas based upon it. He said : " I do
not dispute that 'the enrolment in the State of New York
is erroneous and imperfect,' but I deny, and the Commission has failed to establish, that its errors and imperfec-
tions are greater than those to be found in any other
basis that could be obtained. I do not dispute that ' it
cannot be relied upon as a *just and equitable* basis for the
assignment of quotas ; ' but I assert, and no one can
deny, that no *just* and equitable basis can be found for
the assignment of quotas, and in this war our cause would
be lost if all men stood *exactly* on the order of their going.
* * * The Commission states that the inaccuracies of
the enrolment were a necessary result, under the circumstances, but it fails to show that inaccuracies to an equal
or greater extent would not appear on any other basis.
The Commission seems to have disregarded the fact that
the sources of error were well known to the officers of
this bureau, and that extraordinary pains were taken to
remove them, and it condemns the enrolment after arriving
at certain results by a comparison of the *enrolment of* 1863,
with certain tables prepared by it from the *census of* 1860.
It is not deemed necessary to discuss at length the results
derived from such a comparison. The census of 1860 is
no more likely to have been correct throughout the
country at the time it was taken than the enrolment is
now, * * * but if the census in 1860, and the enrol
ment of 1863, were at those periods equally near correct,
it is unreasonable if not absurd to suppose that the mu-
tations of three years have not added so much to the
inaccuracies of the census of 1860 as to render it at this

time more unreliable and unjust as a basis for quotas than the enrolment of 1863." In relation to the Commission's finding that it was "unable to devise any process or means to correct the enrolment and make it what it should be as a reliable and satisfactory basis for the adjustment of the quota," the Provost Marshal General reported that "if correct, this conclusion of the Commission in connection with what precedes it would of course lead to an entire abandonment of the enrolment, and all action dependent upon it."

The general Government regarded giving up the enrolment at that time as abandoning the reinforcement of the armies, and a surrender to the rebellion. There was no doubt in Washington that the original Enrolment Act contemplated the basing of quotas on the enrolment. If there was doubt elsewhere as to the purpose of Congress it was removed by the amended act approved February 24, 1864, which says the quotas of wards, precincts, etc., "shall be *as nearly as possible* in proportion to the number of *men* resident therein liable to render military service."

The Provost Marshal General insisted "notwithstanding the inability of the Commission to devise any means by which the enrolment can be made what it should be as a reliable basis," that as it stood it was the legal and best basis, and that its material errors could be corrected, and he pointed out the sources of improvement which could be counted on.

Mr. William Whiting, Solicitor of the War Department, said in an official opinion concerning the legality of the enrolment: "The original enrolment was made in pursuance of the Act of March 3, 1863, Chapter 75, and though some names were omitted which should have been added, and other names were inserted which should have been omitted, yet, considering the novelty of the law, the great number of officers acting under it without experience and the magnitude and diffi- culty of the labor they were called on to perform, it is remarkable that the enrolment was so speedily and correctly made."

There were grave objections already indicated, to basing quotas on the census instead of the enrolment. The population to be used for the purpose was that of 1860. If it were a fair basis when made the lapse of three years had effected great changes in it, especially in regard to the men liable to military service. During the first two years of the struggle the States and Districts most ardent in support of the war had sent forward as volunteers a much larger proportion of their men than those States and Districts which opposed or were indif- ferent to the war. To require the former to furnish *from the men remaining* a quota based on the population including those who had gone to the field would have been worse than simple injustice ; it would have been punishing prompt and liberal response to the demands of the Government and rewarding neglect and refusal to comply with those demands. Nevertheless as a conces- sion to Governor Seymour the President, without surren- dering the principle, reduced the quota of New York and disposed of the subject as follows :

"EXECUTIVE MANSION,
WASHINGTON, *February* 27, 1864.

" *Hon. Secretary of War :*

" SIR :—You ask some instructions from me in relation to the Report of special Commission constituted by an

order of the War Department, dated December 5, 1863,
'to revise the enrolment and quotas of the City and
State of New York, and report whether there be any,
and what errors or irregularities therein, and what corrections, if any, should be made.'

"In the correspondence between the Governor of New
York and myself last summer, I understood him to complain that the enrolments in several of the districts of
that State had been neither accurately nor honestly made ;
and in view of this, I, for the draft then immediately ensuing, ordered an arbitrary reduction of the quotas in several
of the districts wherein they seemed too large, and said :
'After this drawing, these four Districts, and also the seventeenth and twenty-ninth, shall be carefully re-enrolled,
and, if you please, agents of yours may witness every
step of the process.' In a subsequent letter I believe
some additional districts were put into the list of those
to be re-enrolled. My idea was to do the work over, according to the law, in presence of the complaining party, and
thereby to correct anything which might be found amiss.
The Commission, whose work I am considering, seem to
have proceeded upon a totally different idea. Not going
forth to find men at all, they have proceeded altogether
upon paper examinations and mental processes. One of
their conclusions, as I understand, is, that as the law
stands, and attempting to follow it, the enrolling officers
could not have made the enrolments much more accurately than they did. The report, on this point, might be
useful to Congress. The Commission conclude that the
quotas for the draft should be based upon entire population, and they proceed upon this basis to give a table for
the State of New York, in which some districts are
reduced and some increased. For the now ensuing draft,

let the quotas stand, as made by the enrolling officers, in the districts wherein the table requires them to be increased; and let them be reduced according to the table in the others: — This to be no precedent for subsequent action; but as I think this report may, on full consideration, be shown to have much that is valuable in it, I suggest that such consideration be given it; and that it be especially considered whether its suggestions can be conformed to without an alteration of the law.

"Yours truly,

"A. LINCOLN."

"Referred to Col. Fry, Provost Marshal General, with directions to make the ensuing draft in New York in conformity with the instructions of the President herein contained.

"EDWIN M. STANTON,

"*Sec.*"

From this time on, the revision of the enrolment was continuously and carefully conducted by the War Department, but without any special aid or co-operation from Governor Seymour, and without further definite complaint from him until a new draft was ordered the following summer.

THE THIRD CALL UNDER THE ENROLMENT ACT, ETC.

The President made a call on the 18th of July, 1864, for 500,000 men, and quotas based on the revised enrolment were distributed. On the 3d of the following month—August—Governor Seymour in a letter to the Secretary of War renewed his opposition to the enrolment and quotas of his State, especially the Cities of New York and Brooklyn. He said: "It is my duty to call

8

your attention to the enrolment made with a view to the draft lately ordered by the President. * * * Since the enrolments were made there has been no opportunity to correct them. Neither can this be done in time. While names may be added to the lists, those which are improperly placed there cannot be stricken off. In large cities the names in excess cannot be detected, as the citizens are not familiar with the names and condition of their neighbors. In the country it is otherwise." Referring to the commission through which the quotas of the preceding year were reduced, he said : " I urge that some similar plan be adopted now, whereby the quotas of this State which, especially in the districts I have named, including New York City and Brooklyn, appear to be unequal and oppressive, may be adjusted equitably in proportion to the demands made in other parts of the country."

Under date of August 10, 1864, the Provost Marshal General reported to the Secretary of War on the matters submitted in the Governor's letter. He showed that the Governor was entirely mistaken in saying " since the enrolments were made there has been no opportunity to correct them ;" that, on the contrary, special opportunities had been afforded to make corrections, commencing as far back as November 17, 1863, when orders were published for that purpose. He added that the Governor was informed of these opportunities, and he quoted a communication issued from the Governor's own headquarters, and signed by his Adjutant-General, embodying the Provost Marshal General's orders of May 18 and 19, 1864, which orders directed that no efforts be spared to revise the enrolment, and that explanation be made to the people of their interest in aiding the revision.

The Governor said in his letter, " if a comparison is made between cities of different States, the disproportion of men demanded from New York and Brooklyn is still more startling. While in these cities *twenty-six* per cent. of the population is enrolled, in Boston only twelve and a half per cent., or less than one-half that ratio, are liable to be drafted."

To this the Provost Marshal General replied : " I am unable to see by what mode of calculation this startling disproportion is arrived at. The population of New York City and Brooklyn, by the last census, is 1,092,791. The enrolment in those cities is 184,925, the percentage of the population which has been enrolled is therefore 16.92. I cannot discover how the Governor can make it 26. The percentage in Boston is correctly given at 12.50 Instead of the ratio of enrolled men to population in Boston being 'less than one half' the same ratio in New York and Brooklyn, it appears that there is a difference of but one quarter between the two. The '*startling*' disproportion, therefore, seems to be founded not altogether upon fact, but partially at least, upon an error in calculation ;" and speaking of the discrepancies which the Governor claimed by comparisons between the enrolment and population, he added, the enrolment " is a mere question of *fact;* it is the ascertainment of the number of men of a certain description in defined areas ; it was made with care, and has been revised with pains on the part of the United States' officers ; and there is no force in the comparisons instituted by the Governor of New York, except so far as they show that the interest taken by the population in perfecting the enrolment is greater in some places than in others." The Provost Marshal General showed further that the enrolment lists were continu-

ously open to revision, and that any name erroneously on
them would be stricken off as soon as the error was
pointed out to the Board of Enrolment by *anybody*. He
also showed that while the quotas of New York were
larger than those of the New England States, they were
smaller than those of New Jersey, much smaller than
those of several of the Western States (where the proportion of men was large), and that they were but 104 men
per congressional district above the average of the
United States ; and he closed by saying : " I can see no
reason why the law should not be applied to New York
as well as to the other States."

The Secretary of War then addressed a letter to Governor Seymour as follows :

> " WAR DEPARTMENT,
> WASHINGTON CITY,
> *August* 11, 1864.

" SIR : In answer to your letter of the 3d instant I have
the honor to submit the report of the Provost Marshal
General, which I trust will satisfy you that the objections
which you have made against the quotas assigned to the
State of New York are not well founded.

" Your communication contains no specification of
unfaithfulness, neglect or misconduct by any enrolling
officer, nor that any errors or mistakes exist in the enrolment but what are unavoidable in making an enrolment
or taking a census. The opportunity for the interested
localities to revise and correct the draft, under the provisions of the law, has been afforded, and will continue
down to the time of the draft. A Commission was appointed last year with a view to ascertain whether any
mistakes or errors had been made by the enrolling
officers ; but the commissioners bore their testimony to

the fidelity with which the work was done. They were of opinion, however, that the basis or principle for the assignment of quotas operated unequally in New York, and, with a view to harmony, the President directed a reduction in some districts, but without the increase of others recommended by the commissioners. The basis for the assignment is now fixed absolutely by act of Congress, and this department has no power to change it.

" In your letter of the 3d inst. it is stated that you ' do not mean to find fault with those who made them (the enrolments) in New York and Brooklyn.'

" It is plain, then, that a Commission could do no more than substitute some other basis of assigning the quota, as was done by the Commission of last year ; and this course would now be contrary to the terms of the statute. A Commission, therefore, would only operate to hinder and delay the Government in strengthening the armies in the field, enable the enemy to protract the war, and expose our arms to disaster and defeat. I do not, therefore, feel authorized to appoint a Commission :

" First.—Because there is ' no fault found ' by you with the enrolling officers, nor any mistake, fraud or neglect on their part alleged by you, requiring investigation by a Commission.

" Second.—The errors of the enrolment, if there be any, can readily be corrected by the Board of Enrolment established by law for the correction of the enrolment.

" Third.—The commission would not have, nor has the Secretary of War, or the President, power to change the basis of the draft prescribed by the Act of Congress.

" Fourth.—The commission would operate to postpone the draft, and perhaps fatally delay strengthening the armies now in the field, thus aiding the enemy and endangering the National Government.

" Every facility will be afforded by this department to correct any error or mistake that may appear in the enrolment, and no effort will be spared to do justice to the Cities of New York and Brooklyn, and apply the law with equality and fairness to every district and in every State.

" I have the honor to be,

" Very respectfully,

" Your obedient servant,

" EDWIN M. STANTON,

" *Secretary of War.*

" TO HIS EXCELLENCY,
   " HORATIO SEYMOUR,
      "GOVERNOR OF NEW YORK, ALBANY."

In his correspondence of 1863 Governor Seymour alleged grievous wrongs—" errors, if they are not shameless frauds," etc.—against the officers of the general Government charged with the enrolment. The request for his full co-operation in making that enrolment was supplemented by applications for his aid in revising it, Mr. Lincoln saying August 7, 1863, " agents of yours may witness every step of the process." In 1864, however, as shown by the letter to which the above is an answer, while still complaining of the result of the enrolment, the Governor acquits the officers whom he had previously accused. He says (letter August 5, 1864, to Secretary of War), " I do not mean to find fault with those who made them in New York and Brooklyn." This revised judgment in 1864, when he was better informed on the subject than in 1863, does not appear in the *Herald* of

1878, the *Times* of 1879, heretofore quoted, nor in the *Twelve Americans* of 1883, which purport to give Governor Seymour's views at present.

The act for enrolment and draft was unpopular and very difficult to execute. It has not been the purpose in this account to apologize for the shortcomings and blunders which attended the administration of it. They are left to the judgment of the impartial historian, who, no doubt, will view them in the light of attending circumstances. Documents enough have been produced, however, to show that Governor Seymour's real opposition was to the law itself, and he was so earnest and persistent in that as to prevent him from being an impartial judge of the manner in which the law was carried out.

In the fall of 1864 the Democratic party lost the State of New York, and on the 1st of January, 1865, Governor Fenton, a Republican, succeeded Governor Seymour.

APPENDIX A.

CHAPTER XII.

THE DRAFT RIOTS OF 1863.

EARLY in July, 1863, Governor Seymour received from General Wool, the United States officer in command of the department, a letter in which he declared that New York City was absolutely without defence from attacks which might be made by rebel gun-boats or ships-of-war, and asked for State troops to hold the harbor fortifications. The communication was a most urgent one. The City of New York was not only the financial centre of the Union, but, to a great extent, the treasury of the nation and storehouse of the Army and Navy. Knowing that such an attack as General Wool feared would be followed by evils, the extent of which no man could estimate, Gov. Seymour, without delay, set about complying with the request made by the representative of the Government, and at the same time determined that he would himself make an inspection of the fortifications. Accompanied by ex-Gov. Morgan and Controller Robison, he did so, and found that General Wool's fears were only too well founded. The so-called defences on the East River and in the harbor were tantamount to no defences at all, and at Throgg's Neck many of the guns commanding the entrance to the city through the Sound were not even mounted. Thoroughly alarmed, and greatly fearing that some adventurous rebel cruiser might obtain information of the city's condition, the Governor, with characteristic energy, gave orders for the transportation of troops from Rochester and other points in the interior to the city fortifications. On Sunday, July 12, while he was at Long Branch and still engaged in this work of providing for the defence of the coast, he was startled by a telegram, informing him that the long-threatened and much-dreaded conscription of men for the Union Army had been commenced in New York City. This telegram was a private one. Gov. Seymour never received any official notification that the draft was to commence, or that it had commenced, nor was any such notification sent to Mr. Opdyke, the Mayor of the City, or to General Wool, the United States officer in command. Without any communication with those gentlemen or with the Department

9

of Police, and without for a moment considering that the forts and arsenals of the city had been stripped of their garrisons, that nearly every volunteer soldier and militiaman in the State had, at the urgent call of the President, been hurried off to the support of Meade and the defence of terror-stricken Pennsylvania, the Provost Marshal—at whose order is to this day a matter of doubt—commenced the draft. The drawing began on Saturday in a district where the enrolment was so excessive, so grossly unjust, that the Government subsequently ordered it to be changed. Most of those whose names came from the wheel were of one nationality, a nationality noted as much for its warm-hearted impulse and reckless generosity as for its tendency to riot and disorder. The names of the conscripts appeared in the papers on Sunday, when they had ample time to meet together and curse the conscription. It has been claimed that there was in all this a deep-seated design for political purposes, to force a portion of the community into such excesses as would make it necessary to declare the Empire City under martial law. This claim has not been justified, but that the Provost Marshals, or those behind them, by their action in the matter, threw prudence, propriety, and common sense to the winds, there can, in view of subsequent events, be no doubt.

Because of his connection with the terrible riots which followed this conscription, managed or mismanaged, as it was, with criminal recklessness, Gov. Seymour has been as severely criticised, and perhaps more bitterly denounced than any public man of his time. It is possible that the following details of that connection, details heretofore known only to a few intimate friends, may cause those who so criticised and denounced him to form a different, and it may be a juster, opinion of his motives and action. On Sunday night, when he first received word that the draft was actually in progress, he tried to make his way to the city, but found that he could not do so. The next morning, at a very early hour, he received a second telegram, informing him that serious disturbances were expected to follow the announcement of the conscription. Fearing the worst, and without having tasted food, he hurried to the metropolis, and, being previously advised, went at once to the St. Nicholas Hotel. Here he found Mayor Opdyke, General Wool, and Mr. Barney, the Collector of the Port, already assembled. Without disparagement to those gentlemen, it may be said that they were more sensible of the danger which threatened the city than they were of any expedient by which it might be averted. They had every reason to be alarmed. A mob, comprising thousands of ruffians maddened by drink, was at large in the streets. The Provost Marshal's office had been sacked, and the block of buildings in which it was situated burned to the ground. The fire-bells tolled out terrible warnings. Clouds of lurid smoke shut out the sun. The authorities were openly defied. Riot ruled the town. No man could say what an hour would bring forth. The very air was filled with untold alarm.

Hardly had the chief magistrate of the State arrived at the St. Nicholas Hotel when the proprietor, fearing that his presence and that of other officers of the law might incite the mob to attack the building, begged him for God's sake to leave it. He and Mayor Opdyke did so. They hastened to the City Hall, and with the scant means at their command, did everything possible to put down the disturbances. The city was declared in a state of insurrection. In order that there might be no conflict between the militia and the police force, which was believed to be unfriendly to the State Government, Mr. Seymour gave to General Ledlie, a Republican, authority to represent him, and to deal with the police and military.

But still the riot went on. Men were shot down in the streets, houses were sacked, and great buildings fell crumbling in flame. A crowd gathered round the City Hall. There were in it quiet, respectable men, and others mad with excitement. The Governor was called upon to speak. Hoping to disperse the mob, desiring to conciliate the good citizens in the crowd, and, above all things, wishing to gain time, protect property, and prevent bloodshed (these were his motives, as he himself has explained them to me), he went boldly before the excited people and implored them to disperse to their homes without further violations of the peace. At the same time he said, according to one report of his short and hurried speech—a report the accuracy of which he has even now no desire to question—" I beg you to listen to me as a friend, for I am your friend and the friend of your families.'' Further than this, he assured them that if they had been wronged in any way, he would use every exertion to see that justice was done them. Then the crowd left the City Hall Square, and from that day to this Horatio Seymour has been by one class of the community denounced for " holding a palaver with bloody criminals " and making "friends" of thieves, cut-throats, and ruffians. Governor Seymour does not desire to reply to these attacks. In vindication of his course, if such vindication be necessary, he simply points to the fact that in forty-eight hours the riots, undoubtedly the most formidable which ever occurred on this continent, were checked and controlled by the State and city authorities without aid from the General Government. In order to accomplish this result it was necessary for the law officers, acting under the authority of the Governor, to shoot down nearly a thousand of the rioters whom he has been accused of " temporizing " with.

Regarding this terrible period in the history of the city, Governor Seymour has long remained silent, but touching the manner in which the riots were suppressed he now authorizes the following statement, which, it may be well

to add, is given in his own words : " The draft riots of 1863 were put down
mainly by the energy, boldness and skill of the Police Department. In saying this I am certainly not influenced by prejudice, for the force was politi-
cally, and, in some degree personally, unfriendly to myself. Indeed, in their
reports they have not seen fit to make mention of any co-operation on my
part with their efforts. But they did their duty bravely and efficiently.
They proved that the City of New York could, by its police alone, in the
absence of its military organizations, cope with the most formidable disorders. I do not know of any instance in history where so many desperate
men were shot down mainly by the police of a city. More than a thousand
of the rioters were killed or wounded to death. Yet so little justice has been
done to the City of New York that many think it was protected by the forces
of the United States. In fact, the Navy-Yard, the vast amount of military
stores of the General Government, and its money in the sub-treasury, were
mainly protected by the civil officers. So protected, while the military organizations of the State were absent in Pennsylvania in answer to an appeal
from the Government of the United States to help it against an invasion of
General Lee. Even General Grant, in one of his papers, spoke of the riot
in New York as an occasion when the General Government had helped State
or local authorities to maintain peace and order. I wrote to him correcting
this error, and it gives me pleasure to say that he received my communication in a spirit of courtesy and of fairness which ever marks the character of
an honorable man. It is now time that justice should be done the City of
New York in this matter, and in the hope that such justice may be done I
repeat these facts."

Before leaving this period in Governor Seymour's life, it will be well to
add that subsequent to the riots, Mr. Watson, then Assistant Secretary of
War, told him that a number of prominent men had made application to
the national administration to place the city under martial law, and that he
(Watson) was sent to New York to see if there was any warrant or necessity
for such action ; that he could find none, and had reported to the department
that Governor Seymour and the civil authorities were doing everything that
could be done to keep the peace.—*New York Times,* 1879.

APPENDIX B.

PROVOST MARSHAL GENERAL'S OFFICE, ⎱
WASHINGTON, D. C. *April* 25, 1863. ⎰

*   *   *   *   *   *   *   *

You will be exclusively under the orders of this Department ; yet, while the Governor of New York has no control over you, you will be required to acquaint yourself with his views and wishes and give them due weight in determining as to the best interests of the General Government of which you are the representative. To this end you will use all proper means to gain and to retain the confidence and good will of the Governor and his State officers. You will endeavor by all means in your power to secure for the execution of the Enrolment Act, the aid and hearty coöperation of His Excellency the Governor; and of the civil officers in his State as also of the people.

*   *   *   *   *   *   *   *

The State of New York has failed to furnish her full quota of men under the President's calls of July 2d, and Aug. 4, 1862, for six hundred thousand men. You will at once calculate by reference to the State records *what proportion* of the deficiency is due to each district under your charge in the State, and inform the Department of the result at the earliest day practicable, * * * taking for the calculation such information in regard to the actual deficiency as the State records may give you.

The enrolment lately made by the State will probably be useful to the Boards in the different districts under your control, and you are therefore desired to have prepared at once and transmitted to them respectively such extracts from the State enrolment lists as will facilitate their business.

*   *   *   *   *   *   *   *

You will take especial care to ascertain and report to this office all cases wherein the Provost Marshals, Surgeons, Commissioners, Enrolling Officers or other employés of this Department shall have proved themselves unworthy or incompetent to fill the positions to which they have been appointed.

*   *   *   *   *   *   *   *

Very respectfully
Your obedient servant,
(*Signed*)   JAMES B. FRY,
Pro.-M'l General.

To COL. ROBERT NUGENT,
,   69TH N. Y. VOLS.

A Letter, in terms as follows, was addressed to Mayor Opdyke :

APPENDIX C.

PROVOST MARSHAL GENERAL'S OFFICE, }
WASHINGTON, D. C., *April* 25, 1863. }

To His Honor, George Opdyke,
Mayor of the City of New York.

SIR :—With a view to uniform and harmonious execution of the Enrolment Act, it has been deemed best to assign an officer of this Department of Rank to duty at the City of New York. He will be instructed to confer with the Governor and yourself, to superintend the operations of the Provost Marshals in the first nine Districts of the State, to secure from the Provost Marshals and Boards in these Districts and submit to the State Executive such rolls and reports as may be deemed necessary for the files of the State, and to prepare from the State Records and transmit to the Provost Marshals and Boards of Enrolment in these districts such information, placed at his disposal by the State authorities as may be necessary or useful to them in the performance of the duties assigned to them. In accordance with the foregoing, Col. Robert Nugent, 69th N. Y. Volunteers, has been directed to take post at New York City. He is an officer of superior ability and a gentleman of attainments, and it is hoped his assignment will prove agreeable to your Honor.

The War Department will be pleased if your Honor will communicate freely with him and secure as far as possible for all officers appointed under the Enrolment Act in these districts the coöperation of the civil officers of your city. I am, Sir,

Very respectfully,
Your obedient servant,
(*Signed*) JAMES B. FRY.
Pro.-M'l General.

APPENDIX D.

(Extract from final report of Provost Marshal General.)

* * * " The paramount duty of the bureau was to complete an enrolment at the earliest practicable date, make it as nearly correct as possible, and under it commence the urgently needed re-enforcement of the armies. The enrolment could be made without injustice to any one, as those who were granted the special favor of exception and exemption from the operations of the act could receive the privilege to which they were entitled after being drafted. To have undertaken so to make the *enrolment* as not to include those who were excused from military service by special enactment, would have been to defeat the purpose of the act, in an attempt as a *first duty* to secure to a privileged class the immunities extended to them before they were ascertained to be due. Supposing all enrolling officers to have been honest and capable, the difficulties and delays they would have met in attempting to decide in advance all cases of exemption which would be presented by persons of the numerous class excepted by the act would have prevented the completion of the enrolment in time to be of use during the war. To this should be added the opposition to be encountered in making an enrolment of any kind, and the fact that the enrollers had, necessarily, to be selected in haste, were but temporarily employed, without power to summon witnesses, and exposed by their irresponsibility and the absence of supervision to the temptation of bribery and favoritism. All this made it clear that the best interests of the Government required that the enrolling officers should not be invested with the power of deciding the questions of exemptions arising under the act. In order, therefore, to get an enrolment for immediate use which, as stated, would be as fair to one place as to another, and which could subsequently be corrected in all places alike, I directed the boards of enrolment to instruct their enrolling officers to enrol all male citizens of the United States, and persons of foreign birth who had declared on oath their intention to become citizens, under and in pursuance of the laws thereof, between the ages of twenty (20) and forty-five (45) years, and not permit the omission from the enrolment lists of the names of persons who might claim to belong to the classes excepted by the law, and to reserve the question of their exemption for consideration after the draft.

" The following extract from a report made by Captain Erhardt, the Provost Marshal of the 4th District, New York City, the enrolment of which was made the subject of special complaint, illustrates the method of making the enrolment, and the pains taken to avoid errors. The mode of operation was not identically the same in all the districts, but varied only according to the circumstances existing in different districts, and the character of the officers and employés engaged in the work. Captain Erhardt says :

' I have the honor to state that there have been enrolled in my district—

' Of first class	54,372
' Of second class	23,405
' Making a total of names enrolled	77,777

' ' From these were taken those who actually lived in this district, and those alone were borne upon the consolidated lists sent to the Provost Marshal General, viz. :—

"Of the first class........................... . 30,844
"Of the second class........................... 11,148

"A total of..................................... 41,992

" ' With this exception that those who were not known to live in any other district, by their own refusal to give their residence, doing business in this, were presumed to live in this, and were sent on the consolidated lists accordingly. These names were in the proportion of, perhaps, one to fifty (1 to 50), so that perhaps eight hundred may be on the consolidated lists so subject to draft here who may show, in case of their being drafted, that they reside in another district, and are not liable. This list, with the deductions of those who reside here, would leave thirty-five thousand seven hundred and eighty-five [35,785] enrolled here not borne upon the consolidated lists of this district.

" ' The enrolment of this district was made by an enrolling officer for each election district, who reported at the headquarters of the district each day with the filled sheets, which were then given in, and an account kept of the amount of sheets (filled) each enrolling officer brought in. The enrolment was completed on the 29th day of June, and the number of names returned to this office amounted to fifty-four thousand three hundred and seventy-two (54,372) of class one, and twenty-three thousand four hundred and five (23,405) of class two ; total number, seventy-seven thousand seven hundred and seventy-seven (77,777).

" ' The consolidation was made by first making an alphabetical list of each ward ; the names were carefully revised, and the residence of every person, within the ages named in the act, residing in this district, marked by the ward of this district in which he resided. They were then transferred to another copy, care being taken to gather all who resided in the ward, copying from other wards. On the completion of that copy the lists were again revised for the purpose of ascertaining duplicates, in this manner : by taking the first name of each letter and going through all the rest of the letter, to ascertain that that name was down but once; then taking the second name, and again going through those remaining, until the whole had undergone a careful and actual scrutiny ; and in the same manner with class two. This was the work of many days and nights, yet it resulted in a correct list. When a doubt arose as to whether the party under search was a duplicate, an enrolling officer was sent to the residence of such a party to ascertain whether such name was a duplicate or not.

" ' Upon the completion of that copy another copy was made, and all errors stricken from and transfers made, should any be found in it. After a careful revision of that copy the final copy was made for the department, and from that the cards prepared for the draft, and carefully compared with the list, and verified by actual count.'

" Numerous and weighty obstacles were encountered in making this enrolment. The large floating population of the country, and the disposition and right of our people to go from place to place without let or hindrance, rendered it exceedingly difficult to perfect it. Most of the embarrassments resulted, however, from the opposition encountered in almost every house, if not to the act itself, at least to its application to the particular persons whose names were sought for enrolment. The law made it the duty of this bureau to *take*, but did not make it the duty of any one to *give*, the names of those liable to draft. Every imaginable artifice was adopted to deceive and defeat the enrolling officers. Open violence was sometimes met with. Several enrollers lost their lives. Some were crippled. The property of others was destroyed to intimidate them and prevent the enrolment. In certain mining regions organized bodies of men openly opposed the enrolment, rendering it necessary that the United States authorities should send troops to overcome their opposition. There were secret societies, newspapers and politicians who fostered and encouraged this widespread opposition.

" Under these serious drawbacks the first enrolment was made. It was no more imperfect than had been expected, and the first draft (as explained hereafter in this report) was, according to it, conducted in such a manner as to neutralize to a great extent (if not entirely) the irregularities and hardships that might have resulted from the errors it contained."

APPENDIX E.

ELMIRA, *May* 22, 1863.

Colonel James B. Fry,
Provost Marshal General.

COLONEL:—I have just returned from Albany where I had a protracted audience with Governor Seymour. My attention—as yours must have been—had been attracted to his remarkable letter to the meeting at the Capitol the preceding evening, denouncing the proceeding against Valandingham. This letter was of course the subject of conversation. My personal relations with the Governor having always been friendly, and much of the conversation having been confidential in its character, I hardly know how to communicate to

10

you regarding it. I feel authorized, however, to say that the Governor will co-operate with the General Government in such measures as may be adopted for raising armies and carrying on the war. He thinks the question of constitutionality of the law will be raised, but says that is a question for the courts. He wanted me to understand and to communicate to the President that he was exceedingly tenacious in relation to the question of arbitrary arrests. I referred him to the law of Congress upon this subject as contained in the Act authorizing the suspension of the writ of *habeas corpus* and the Act relating to the draft. I understood him to be content if arrests were made in compliance with those provisions, and if my advice were of any value I would suggest that these laws be respected, as they were framed after a great deal of consideration and had the support of the best minds in Congress.

 * * * * * * *

I have the honor to be

Your obedient Servant,

(*Signed*)   A. S. DIVEN,

A. A. P. M. Gen'l.

P. S.—I would thank you to show the Secretary of War so much of this letter at least as relates to my interview with Governor Seymour.

APPENDIX F.

A. A. P. M. GEN'L'S OFFICE,
ELMIRA, N. Y.,
July 23, 1863.

Colonel James B. Fry,
 Provost Marshal General.

COLONEL :—I understand the position of Governor Seymour in relation to the draft to be this. That any drafted man has a right to the writ of *habeas corpus ;* that if the military authorities refuse to produce a man held by them as a drafted man, and to abide the decision of the Judge, that then he would employ all the power vested in him as Governor, including, of course, his military power as Commander-in-chief of the Militia of the State, to secure the right.

Now I assume that the Governor is sincere, when he says if the law is declared by the courts to be constitutional, then all his power shall be used for its enforcement. How can the adjudication be had without embarrassing delay? is the question. Of course the tribunal of last resort is the one to appeal to, before this could be said to be definitely declared.

I propose this—either of the Justices of the Supreme Court of the United States can issue the writ of *habeas corpus.* Let application for a writ be at once made to each of the Judges for the discharge of a drafted man, and on the question of granting or denying the writ, the Justices can separately give their opinions, and thus within a few days the mind of the Court can be ascertained.

There can be no doubt surely about the decision. I at least have not the legal discernment to appreciate any point that has been made against the validity of the law. This proposition I would make to Governor Seymour if authorized, and it would certainly test the sincerity of his profession, and would fulfil the pledges he has made to the men complaining of the law.

I have the honor to be

Your obedient servant,

(*Signed*) A. S. DIVEN,

A. A. P. M. Gen'l. W. D., N. Y.

APPENDIX G.

BUFFALO, NEW YORK,

August 6, 1863.

His Excellency Horatio Seymour,

Governor of New York.

DEAR SIR:—As I promised you I would, I visited Washington and conferred with the authorities relative to the subject of our conversation. The executive officers of the Government in execution of the laws of Congress will do nothing to assume that these laws are invalid, particularly as in this case they entertain no doubts as to the constitutionality of the law providing for the draft. They would be glad at the same time where doubts exist to have the parties entertaining them satisfied without embarrassing the operations of the Government.

The course suggested at our personal interview, to reach an adjudication that should be final and satisfactory, is the only one that occurs to me and I hope will be resorted to.

On application for the writ of *habeas corpus* directly to one of the Justices of the Supreme Court, if the applicant simply states the ground for applying for the writ to be the invalidity of the law under which he is held, the Justice would in granting or denying the writ, have but the single question to pass upon and would if counsel was to be heard give time and place for hearing. The question can thus be put at rest, and I sincerely hope you will advise this course to be adopted by those who want to contest the validity of this

Act of Congress, as I should regret to have anything occur in the State of New York that could delay the reinforcement of an army composed so largely of her own devoted men.

I am, Governor, very sincerely,

Your obedient servant,

(*Signed*)   A. S. DIVEN,

A. A. P. M. G., W. D., N. Y.

APPENDIX H.

HEADQUARTERS CITY AND HARBOR OF NEW YORK,   ⎱
CITY OF NEW YORK, *July* 28, 1863.   ⎰

The General-in-Chief,
  Washington, D. C.

SIR:—I have the honor to acknowledge the receipt of your communication of yesterday.   Assuming, as in my judgment we should, that the enforcement of the draft will be resisted and that this resistance may take the form of an insurrection against the General Government, it will be prudent to re-inforce the troops now here to such an extent as will secure the forts in the harbor against any sudden seizure by the mob or by insurgents.

The volunteer recruits in this neighborhood and the State militia furnish in numbers a sufficient force for this purpose, but it is still questionable how far the local troops may be relied on in the event of an outbreak. The State authorities have not yet declared themselves with sufficient distinctness to deprive the disaffected of all hope of sympathy if not of assistance in any movement they may undertake, and it is to be apprehended that they may not do this until it is too late.   If the proper course is adopted by them there will be no serious trouble. If it is not there will be, and it will not be safe to allow the control of the harbor to depend in any degree upon this chance.

I think the minimum force required for this purpose will be four regiments of infantry of medium strength—2,000 or 2,400 men—and they should be drawn from the troops that will not sympathize with any local excitement, as that will enable us to employ without danger some portion of the volunteer recruits now in this neighborhood.

The contingency may not occur, and in that case the troops may soon be returned, but the lesson will not be thrown away.

Very respectfully, Sir,

Your obedient servant,

(*Signed*)   ED. R. S. CANBY,

Brig.-Genl. Comd'g.

APPENDIX I.

HEADQUARTERS DEPARTMENT OF THE EAST, }
NEW YORK CITY, *August* 12, 1863. }

Hon. Edwin M. Stanton,
    Secretary of War,

    *   *   *   *   *   *   *

SIR :—I am constrained to believe that the whole moral influence of the executive power of the State will be thrown against the execution of the law for enrolling and calling out the national forces, and a case may occur in which the military power of the State will be employed to defeat it.

    *   *   *   *   *   *   *

I have the honor to be
    Very respectfully yours,
(*Signed*)   JOHN A. DIX,
                Major-General.

APPENDIX J.

NEW YORK, *August* 12, 1863

Colonel James B. Fry,
    Provost Marshal General.

I was in consultation last evening with General Canby, the Mayor and Police Commissioners. We are of opinion that the draft can safely commence in this city on Monday with a sufficient force, but there ought to be ten thousand troops in the city and harbor. General Canby has now five thousand. Governor Seymour's letters have increased the disaffection and multiplied the chances of collision, and there is little doubt that he will do all in his power to defeat the draft, short of forcible resistance to it. I will write the Secretary of War fully by to-day's mail.

    (*Signed*),   JOHN A. DIX,
                Major General.

APPENDIX K.

HEADQUARTERS DEPARTMENT OF THE EAST, {
NEW YORK CITY, *July* 30, 1863. {

His Excellency, Horatio Seymour,
  Governor of the State of New York.

SIR :—As the draft under the Act of Congress of March 3, 1863, for enrolling and calling out the national forces will probably be resumed in this city at an early day, I am desirous of knowing whether the military power of the State may be relied on to enforce the execution of the law in case of forcible resistance to it. I am very anxious that there should be perfect harmony of action between the Federal Government and that of the State of New York ; and if under your authority to see the laws faithfully executed, I can feel assured that the act referred to will be enforced, I need not ask the War Department to put at my disposal for the purpose troops in the service of the United States.

I am the more unwilling to make such a request, as they could not be withdrawn in any considerable number from the field, without prolonging the war and giving aid and encouragement to the enemies of the Union at the very moment when our successes promise, with a vigorous effort, the speedy suppression of the rebellion.

I have the honor to be
Very respectfully,
Your obedient Servant,
JOHN A. DIX,
Major General.

APPENDIX L.

HEADQUARTERS DEPARTMENT OF THE EAST, {
NEW YORK, *August* 8, 1863. {

His Excellency, Horatio Seymour,
  Governor of the State of New York.

SIR : — I had the honor to receive on the evening of the 5th inst. your letter of the 3d, in reply to mine of the 30th ult., informing me that you had made a communication to the President of the United States in relation to the draft in this State, and expressing your belief that his answer would relieve you and me "from the painful questions growing out of an armed enforcement of the Conscription Act," etc.

Your Excellency promises to write me again on the subject when you shall have received the President's answer. It will afford me great pleasure to hear from you and to receive an affirmative answer to the inquiry contained in my letter. But I owe it to my position as Commander of this Military Department, to anticipate his reply by some suggestions arising out of your answer to me.

You are no doubt aware that the draft has been nearly completed in the nine western districts, and that it also has been completed in several districts ; and is in successful progress in others in the central part of the State, under the orders of Provost Marshal General.

It is my duty now as Commanding Officer of the troops in the service of the United States in the Department if called on by the enrolling officers, to aid them in resisting forcible opposition to the execution of the law; and, it was from an earnest desire to avoid the necessity of employing, for the purpose, any of my forces, which have been placed here to garrison the forts and protect the public property, that I wished to see the draft enforced by the military power of the State, in case of an armed and organized resistance to it. But holding such resistance to the paramount law of Congress to be disorganizing and revolutionary, leading, unless effectually suppressed, to the overthrow of the Government itself, to the success of the insurgents in the seceded States, and to universal anarchy, I designed, if your co-operation could not be relied on, to ask the General Government for a force which should be adequate to ensure the execution of the law, and to meet any emergency growing out of it.

The Act under which the draft is in progress, was, as your Excellency is aware, passed to meet the difficulty of keeping up the army, through the system of volunteering, to the standard of force deemed necessary to suppress the insurrection. The service of every man capable of bearing arms is, in all countries, those especially in which power is responsible to the people, due to the Government when its existence is in peril. This service is the price of the protection which he receives, and of the safeguards with which the law surrounds him in the enjoyment of his property and life. The Act authorizing the draft is entitled, " An Act for enrolling and calling out the national forces." I regret that your Excellency should have characterized it as " The Conscription Act." A phrase borrowed from a foreign system of enrolment, with odious features from which ours is wholly free, and originally applied to the law in question by those who desired to bring it into reproach and defeat its execution. I impute to your Excellency no such purpose. On the contrary, I assume it to have been altogether inadvertent ;

but I regret it, because there is danger that in thus designating it and deprecating "an armed enforcement" of it, you may be understood to regard it as an obnoxious law, which ought not to be carried into execution, thus throwing the influence of your high position against the Government in a conflict for its existence.

The call which has been made for service is for one-fifth part of the arms-bearing population, between 20 and 35 years of age, and of the unmarried between 35 and 45. The insurgent authorities at Richmond have not only called into service heretofore the entire class between 18 and 35, but are now extending the enrolment to classes more advanced in age. The burden which the loyal States are called on to sustain is not, in proportion to population, one-tenth part as onerous as that which has been assumed by the seceded States. Shall not we, if necessary, be ready to do as much for the preservation of our political institutions as they are doing to overthrow and destroy them; as much for the cause of stable government as they for the cause of treason and for the disorganization of society on this continent? I say the disorganization of society, for no man of reflection can doubt where secession would end if a Southern Confederacy should be successfully established.

I cannot doubt that the people of this patriotic State, which you justly say has done so much for the country during the existing war, will respond to the call now made upon them. The alacrity and enthusiasm with which they have repeatedly rushed to arms for the support of the Government and the defence of the national flag from insult or degradation, have exalted the character and given new vigor to the moral power of the State, and will inspire our descendants with magnanimous resolutions for generations to come. This example of fidelity to all that is honorable and elevated in public duty must not be tarnished.

The recent riots in this city, coupled as they were with the most atrocious and revolting crimes, have cast a shadow over it for the moment. But the promptitude with which the majesty of the law was vindicated, and the fearlessness with which a high judicial functionary is pronouncing judgment upon the guilty, have done, and are doing much to efface what, under a different course of action, might have been an indelible stain upon the reputation of the city. It remains only for the people to vindicate themselves from reproach in the eyes of the country and the world by a cheerful acquiescence in the law. That it has defects is generally conceded. That it will involve cases of personal hardship is not disputed. War, when waged for self-defence, for the maintenance of great principles, and for the national life, is not exempt from the sufferings inseparable from all conflicts which are decided by the shock of armies, and it is by our firmness and our patriotism in meeting all the calls of the country upon us, that we achieve the victory and prove ourselves worthy of it and the cause in which we toil and suffer.

Whatever defects the act authorizing the enrolment and draft may have, it is the law of the land, framed in good faith by the representatives of the people, and it must be presumed to be consistent with the provisions of the Constitution until pronounced in conflict with them by competent judicial tribunals. Those therefore, who array themselves against it are *obnoxious* to far severer censure than the ambitious or misguided men who are striving to subvert the Government ; for, the latter are acting by color of sanction under legislatures and conventions of the people in the States they represent. Among us, resistance to the law by those who claim and enjoy the protection of the Government has no semblance of justification and becomes the very blackest of political crimes, not only because it is revolt against the constituted authorities of the country, but because it would be practically striking a blow for treason, and arousing to new efforts and new crimes, those who are staggering to their fall under the resistless power of our recent victories.

In conclusion, I renew the expression of my anxiety to be assured by your Excellency at the earliest day practicable, that the military power of the State will, in case of need, be employed to enforce the draft. I desire to receive the assurance, because under a mixed system of government like ours, it is best that resistance to the law should be put down by the authority of the State in which it occurs. I desire it also, because I shall otherwise deem it my duty to call on the General Government for a force which shall not only be adequate to insure the execution of the law, but which shall enable me to carry out such decisive measures as shall leave their impress upon the mind of the country for years to come.

I have the honor to be,

Very respectfully, yours,

JOHN A. DIX,
Major General.

II

APPENDIX M.

HEADQUARTERS DEPARTMENT OF THE EAST, }
NEW YORK CITY, *August* 10, 1863.

Col. Jas. B. Fry,
    Provost Marshal General.
COLONEL:
    *   *   *   *   *   *   *

I have asked the Governor whether I can rely on his co-operation with the military power of the State. He has not answered. The President's letter to him, which I have seen this morning, is admirable, and I do not see how he can avoid giving an affirmative answer to my inquiry.
    *   *   *   *   *   *   *
    I am, respectfully yours,

JOHN A. DIX,
Major General.

———

APPENDIX N.

HEADQUARTERS DEPARTMENT OF THE EAST, }
NEW YORK CITY, *August* 18, 1863.

His Excellency, Horatio Seymour,
    Governor of the State of New York.

SIR :—I did not receive until last evening your letter of the 15th instant. Immediately on my arrival in this city on the 18th ult., I called upon you with General Canby, and in a subsequent interview with you at my headquarters, I expressed the wish that the draft in this State should be executed without the employment of the troops in the service of the United States. In a letter addressed to you on the 30th ult., I renewed more formally the expression of this wish, and stated that if the military power of the State could be relied on to enforce the draft, in case of forcible resistance to it, I need not call on the Secretary of War for troops for the purpose.

In the same spirit when some of the Provost Marshals in the interior applied to me for aid against threatened violence, I referred them to you in order that they might be protected by your authority. It was my earnest wish that the Federal arm should neither be seen nor felt in the execution of the law for enrolling and calling out the national forces, but that it might be carried out under the *ægis* of the State, which has so often been interposed between the General Government and its enemies. Not having received an answer from you, I applied to the Secretary of War on the 14th inst. for a force adequate to the object.

The call was promptly responded to, and I shall be ready to meet all opposition to the draft. I trust, however, that your determination, of which your letter advises me, to call into requisition the military power, if need be, to put down violations of good order, riotous proceedings, and disturbances of the public peace, as infractions of the laws of this State, will render it unnecessary to use the troops under my command for that purpose, and that their only service here may be to protect the public property and the officers of the U. S. in the discharge of their duties, and to give those who intend to uphold the Government, as well as those who are seeking to subvert it, the assurance that its authority will always be firmly and effectually maintained.

I am, very respectfully,
Your obedient servant,
JOHN A. DIX,
Major General.

APPENDIX O.

NEW YORK CITY, N. Y.,
August 18, 1863.

Maj. Gen'l Halleck,
General-in-chief

* * * * * * *

Governor Seymour, at the last moment, has notified me that there can be no violation of good order, no riotous proceedings, and no disturbances of the public peace which are not infractions of laws of the State ; that those laws will be enforced under all circumstances.

JNO. A. DIX,
Maj. Gen'l.

APPENDIX P.

WASHINGTON, D. C.,
July 29, 1863. 2.30 P.M.

Major General Meade,
Army of Potomac.

As it is quite possible that we may be obliged to detach some of your troops to enforce the draft and to bring on the drafted men, I think it would be best to hold for the present the upper line of the Rappahannock without further pursuit of Lee. I will telegraph you as soon as I can get a decision in regard to the 11th Corps.

H. W. HALLECK,

General-in-chief.

APPENDIX Q.

HEADQUARTERS ARMY OF POTOMAC, }

(10:30 A.M.)   *August* 16, 1863. }

Major General H. W. Halleck,

    General-in-Chief.

The following regiments will proceed to Alexandria to-day under the command of Brig. General T. H. Ruger, viz.: 2d Massachusetts, 3d Wisconsin, 27th Indiana, 5th Ohio, 7th Ohio, 29th Ohio, 66th Ohio, 4th Ohio, 14th Indiana, 5th Michigan, 126th Ohio. The aggregate strength of these regiments is about 3,800. General Ruger has been directed to report to you by telegraph on arriving at Alexandria for further instructions, and also by telegraph to the Quartermaster General for transportation. The number of men detached and who have left are as follows:

August 14th, Regulars and Vermont Brigade, under General Ayers, 4,000.

August 15th, Regiments, 1,400.

August 16th, Ruger's command 3,800: making in all 9,200, which, when swollen by convalescents, and men detached on extra duty, who will be sent as soon as possible, will make the aggregate force fully up to and over 10,000. I do not propose without further orders to send any more. I have sent you my best troops and some of my best officers.

GEO. G. MEADE,

Major General Comd'g.

APPENDIX R.

"OPINION."

"The position taken by the Governor of New York is not regarded as sustained either by the letter or spirit of the Enrolment Act. The State in which a drafted man is enrolled is necessarily credited with one soldier, whether such drafted man enters the service personally or furnishes a substitute, or pays the commutation money. If such person employs a substitute and that substitute chances to be from another State, then this latter State, according to the Governor's view, must also be credited with one soldier, so that the practical operation of the rule would be to credit the Government with two soldiers, when, in fact, it receives but one. Such an interpretation should not be allowed to prevail, since it has no foundation in reason, and is in derogation of the leading object of the Enrolment Act, which is to provide an army for the public defence—an object that would be but illy accomplished if, in the computation, one soldier is to be counted to the Government as two.

" J. HOLT,

" *Judge Advocate General.*"

August 24, 1863.

www.ingramcontent.com/pod-product-compliance
Lightning Source LLC
Chambersburg PA
CBHW031450270326
41930CB00007B/930